EMPOWERED
AT A DISTANCE

HOW TO BUILD STUDENT SELF-DIRECTION INTO REMOTE AND HYBRID LEARNING

WRITTEN AND ILLUSTRATED BY
DR. JOHN SPENCER

Empowered at a Distance: How to Build Student Self-Direction into Remote and Hybrid Learning

Copyright © 2020 by John Spencer

BLEND

Blend Education
PO Box 5953
Salem, OR 97304

Paperback ISBN: 978-1-7341725-9-1

eBook ISBN: 978-1-7341726-0-7

CONTENTS

CHAPTER 1

TEACHING AMID
UNCERTAINTY

I'm standing in the kitchen, staring aimlessly at the cupboard. Though it's only three weeks into the quarantine, I'm officially at the "thinking way too hard to about whether black beans or pinto beans will work best in a burrito" stage of social isolation.

My daughter barrels down the stairs and startles me. "Hey, Dad, I just want to make sure we have the correct route."

"What route?" I ask.

"For the parade. Can you doublecheck that for me?"

I vaguely remember the email, but honestly, it had slipped my mind. But not my daughter's. This will be the highlight of her day. She's been looking forward to this from the moment she woke up. Apparently, she has read and re-read the email from her teacher, but she's terrified of missing out on a critical detail.

I pull out my phone and review the parade route with her. Half an hour later, we step out onto our front yard. All around us, crowds of families gather on their front decks and porches. Several of the kids are holding hand-painted signs.

From a distance, we hear the horns honking and the occasional blip of a siren.

The whole block buzzes in eager anticipation. Kids shout out to their siblings as more children stream out of their homes and onto their lawns. Eventually, the parade snakes through our neighborhood, their cars decorated with bright balloons and streamers and positive messages. My daughter waves at the teachers, the aides, the custodians, the cafeteria workers, and the librarian.

The principal waves and calls out my daughter by name – something she does for every child she sees. Her voice is hoarse from saying their names, but she keeps going. Tears well up in my eyes as my daughter says "goodbye" one last time to her teacher. We may be experiencing isolation, but right now, my daughter feels known.

I glance over a few houses away and notice two high-school students (keeping their respectful social distance) who have come out of their homes with signs thanking their former teachers who have made a profound difference in their lives. One of them holds a sign that reads, "I wouldn't have gotten into college without you."

These two seniors have lost their senior prom, their senior play, their spring sports, their goofy senior pranks, and even their graduation because of this pandemic. They are likely grieving the loss of these once-in-a-lifetime events. However, here they are, standing outside, carrying signs thanking the teachers and staff who have changed their world forever.

I would say that I'm surprised by the parade and the cheers and the reaction from the families around me. But none of this is surprising. Even though the job can feel thankless at times, this moment in quarantine is making visible a reality we know to be true. Teachers make a profound difference, regardless of the subject or grade or even format of the teaching.

This period of quarantine has proven that teachers care deeply about their students. I've seen so many examples of teachers making phone calls to families, having class video conferences, and going out of their way to make sure kids know that there's another adult out there who cares. I've seen third-grade teachers doing read-alouds and high-school teachers writing positive notes to seniors.

At the university level, I am watching professors eagerly learning how to use virtual learning strategies so they can continue to connect with their students. Professors all around me are making phone calls to students to see how students are doing mentally and emotionally. Many of these instructors have gone out of their way to find resources for adult learners who were struggling with the shift in course format. Other professors are connecting with local agencies for students who are experiencing trauma. It is a bold reminder that in higher education, professors might be experts in a specific field or domain, but they are also deeply dedicated to their classroom community.

This sudden shift toward emergency pandemic teaching has also been a reminder that teaching is inherently relational, and educators at every level care deeply about those they serve.

In the initial quarantine phase, schools mobilized in a matter of days to support students and families. At breakneck speed, principals and district office leaders managed this transition quickly, often with patience and empathy, to provide resources and training to make teaching work. Cafeteria and food service staff mobilized in a matter of a few days to ensure that students had access to a free breakfast and lunch every day during this crisis. Schools launched laptop rollouts and sent school buses to neighborhoods to provide free Wi-Fi. I watched tech directors and specialists work twelve-hour days making sure students had access to the tools they needed. Counselors and social workers networked with families and agencies to continue to provide vital care for students.

None of this is surprising to teachers. It's what they do. However, in the past, we've seen media reports scapegoat teachers for having low academic standards and praising reformers who were going to use high-stakes tests to "hold teachers accountable."

Teachers have endured the negative stereotypes. When I taught eighth grade, I bit my tongue when folks would say, "Must be nice to have summers off." On several occasions, I had someone quote the snarky cliché, "Those who can, do. Those who can't, teach." There were moments when I wondered if society actually appreciated our tireless work at all. Toward the end of the summer, the snark returned, with media personalities mocking teachers who were uncomfortable going back to face-to-face instruction.

However, for all the snark and negativity that has been directed toward educators from a vocal minority in the media, the parade was a reminder of the sheer importance of teachers.

TEACHERS

HAVE ALREADY PROVEN THAT

SOCIAL DISTANCE

DOESN'T HAVE TO MEAN

RELATIONAL DISTANCE

WHAT SOCIETY LEARNED
ABOUT EDUCATORS

This period of pandemic pedagogy has proven that teachers care deeply about their students. If you hopped onto social media in the spring of the quarantine, you would have seen teachers grieving for the things that they would miss. No field day. No end of the year party. No graduation. No epic project that they were saving for the end. For professors, it meant missing out on cohort celebrations and the beauty of watching first-generation college students standing on the stage with their diploma, waving at their parents who worked tirelessly to create this opportunity.

It goes much deeper than that. If you stepped into the staff video conference, you would have seen teachers sharing concerns about specific kids in potentially unsafe spaces. You would have seen them finding creative solutions to help their students access the lessons and remain connected to the classroom community. If you'd visited a community college department meeting, you might have seen professors working through specific plans to help some of the most vulnerable students avoid slipping through the cracks.

This response wasn't about pity, either. It was an empathy rooted in relationships. Teachers have been partnering with parents to make education work for specific families. I love the fact that we got a phone call from my daughter's teacher checking in on us and making sure we had technology and Wi-Fi but also asking about any other systemic support they could offer. I appreciated how quick my oldest son's teacher was to raise a concern when he failed to turn in his assignments. During these chaotic times, teachers provided choices for students. They allowed for flexible deadlines. They found ways to keep the work challenging and engaging.

The pandemic has revealed just how innovative teachers could be. Call it adaptable or resourceful if "innovation" isn't your term. But it has been a grassroots mobilization. I've watched teachers form small groups using video conferencing, walkie-talkie apps, and social media where they check in on one another and problem-solve the challenges they are facing. I'm in a mastermind group right now where folks have been sharing strategies for increasing student engagement in video conferencing. I'm part of three different private Facebook groups where we share resources back and forth. Log into Twitter and you'll see all kinds of chats where teachers are asking, "What does it mean to teach well from a distance?" They're having hard conversations about equity and asking what it means to teach in a culturally responsive way online.

The context is changing rapidly, and the policies are still lagging behind at times. However, throughout this pandemic, teachers have been planning, implementing, revising, and iterating at a rapid speed. It's been pretty amazing.

But this phase was merely emergency remote learning. Teachers and professors did a phenomenal job creating meaningful learning experiences despite having limited resources and a short time frame. By necessity, educators have had to be reactive rather than proactive. This initial period of pandemic pedagogy revealed some distinct challenges to remote learning and unearthed some critical inequities in our systems.

THE CHALLENGE OF DISENGAGEMENT

In every context, from kindergarten through graduate school, instructors faced a huge challenge in student engagement. Part of this was rooted in inequity. Students failed to log in to the learning management system (LMS) or attend virtual meetings due to a lack of technology access. Some students were sharing devices with siblings or battling painfully slow internet connections. In other cases, students were experiencing trauma and navigating a chaotic situation at home. Adolescents were suddenly taking care of younger siblings because their parents were deemed essential workers.

Meanwhile, university students were facing an uncertain job market while also losing their jobs in the service industry. Those living on campus were suddenly stuck trying to find alternative housing. In some cases, students could not access the learning because they lacked key accommodations that they needed as exceptional learners. In these moments, disengagement was the result of injustice. In this book, we will devote an entire chapter to the theme of access and equity. We can't focus on self-direction and empowerment without first focusing on equity and access.

In other cases, students were confused by course design and layout. They had a hard time navigating tasks and understanding expectations. For this reason, we will address course design and layout in chapter 14. Other times, students struggled with isolation and felt distant from their classmates. This is why we will devote a chapter to community building and we'll focus on how to build student ownership into virtual meetings.

But even when instructors designed quality assignments and lessons, certain students seemed to lack initiative and self-direction. This is why our book centers on empowering students. At the heart of this book are three big truths.

BIG TRUTH #1
THE PROBLEM OF ENGAGEMENT STARTS WITH EMPOWERMENT

The lack of student engagement is often a lack of self-direction. When schools shift to remote-learning courses, certain students who would normally do well in person end up struggling to manage their time and get started on their learning. They get distracted and fail to develop deep work habits that can lead to success. Here, students might even fail to show up to class video conferences or respond to emails. They turn in work significantly late and at a lower quality than they would if they were in a physical classroom. Without the teacher present and the reminder of accountability, these students disengage.

But this issue is less about engagement and more about empowerment. In some of these courses, instructors design highly engaging activities and curate relevant materials and still experience lower student engagement. Ultimately, students have to take the initiative to own their learning when the teacher isn't physically present. As educators, we cannot beat ourselves up over lower engagement. However, we can choose to grow and improve in our distance learning journey. We can create systems and structures that empower students to own the learning process. We can design collaborative structures that encourage interdependency and mutual accountability. We can tap into student interests and curiosity in a way that affirms their agency. We can provide choice and flexibility in assignments and craft distance learning projects that promote student voice and creativity. We can empower students to self-select their scaffolds to help ensure accessibility. We can engage students in authentic self-assessment and peer assessment using synchronous and asynchronous tools.

There is no guarantee that every student will be engaged in the learning process. However, we can design experiences that empower students and boost ownership. For this reason, each chapter will be oriented around a key area of student empowerment and self-direction.

BIG TRUTH #2
IT'S NOT ABOUT THE TECH

As educators shift toward remote and hybrid learning, there is a tendency to focus on specific technology tools. What hardware do we purchase? What apps do we need? What learning management platform works best? But this approach is a bit like building a house by selecting materials and tools without drawing up a blueprint or thinking strategically about the needs of the homeowner.

A tech-centered approach can create mismatches between the learning tasks and the tools students are using. This is what happens when a school purchases a set of video cameras for every classroom and requires teachers to livestream lessons for students at home without asking about the intended learning outcomes and the needs of students. An educator implementing a learner-centered approach would ask, "What do we want students to learn?" and then focuses on the question "What are the best tools and platforms that allow students to learn in person and at home?" Thus, instead of live-streaming lessons, a teacher might have some prerecorded videos, materials, small-group video chats, and choice menus.

Tech-centric solutions promise fast, convenient, and efficient learning outcomes. Adaptive learning programs promise to deliver personalized content at each student's level. Just log on and let the algorithm work its magic. Districts have spent millions of dollars on comprehensive online curriculum with handouts that students can print, fill out, and scan from home. In some cases, universities have even experimented with AI instructors who will answer student questions on-demand. However, these solutions fail to engage students in creativity, critical thinking, or collaboration.

Teachers are the guides that encourage and inspire critical thinking. They are the architects designing deeper learning. They are the leaders of a classroom community. The sheer number of kids outside cheering during our neighborhood parade was a reminder that teaching isn't about content delivery. It's about relationships.

Ultimately, the teachers who thrive in remote learning won't necessarily be the ones who know the apps inside and out. They will be the ones who know their students, their subjects, and their crafts. This doesn't mean you should avoid technology or fail to learn about various apps and platforms. Schools need technology expertise. But this expertise should be centered on student learning. As you read this book, you'll notice that I don't provide specific instructions for how to use technology. I rarely mention the names of specific apps. Each school, district, and university has a different set of tools that work best for them. Instead, this book will focus on specific teaching and learning strategies and how these apply to remote and hybrid learning.

BIG TRUTH #3
THERE IS NO INSTRUCTION MANUAL.

There is no single right way to do remote and hybrid teaching. Every context is different. Some teachers will lean heavily into virtual chats, while others will use mostly asynchronous tools. Some professors will stick to a comprehensive LMS while others use an assortment of tools with the LMS acting as a single hub or springboard. In some subject areas, instructors will focus on multimedia composition, while others focus more heavily on reading and writing. Some hybrid courses will combine small groups that are both in person and at home. In other courses, the instructor will run things on a two-track system with in-person and at-home groups attending the same synchronous lessons.

Every class is different. This why there is no instruction manual for remote and hybrid learning. Although this book presents practical strategies and a general blueprint for increasing student ownership, it does not offer a formula or recipe for empowering students. I cannot promise 100% student engagement at all times if you follow specific steps. In fact, I can almost guarantee that you will have lessons that fail miserably as you move through this distance-learning journey.

Right now, things might feel unpredictable. However, teaching has always been unpredictable. Every year means a new group of students with a new set of desires, needs, and skills. Each course has a different climate and culture. We can't predict what this next semester will hold. However, we can be strategic and proactive by designing systems that will increase student ownership.

THERE IS NO
INSTRUCTION MANUAL
FOR DISTANCE LEARNING

BUT THERE ARE BLUEPRINTS

The shift toward remote learning is an experiment, and it varies depending on your subject, your context, and your students. You'll make tons of mistakes — and that's okay. The beauty is in learning from those mistakes so you can iterate and improve your instruction. Lean into the experts in your own institution and be humble about what you don't know. Ask students for their input and refine your approach along the way. Over time, you'll develop some amazing distance learning experiences.

When you view remote learning as an experiment, it can change your definition of success. For years, schools have focused on student achievement scores as the metric defining teacher success. But when we admit that teaching is unpredictable and remote learning is experimental, we can redefine success. Instead of focusing on external outcomes, we can define success as humbly admitting what didn't work and choosing to grow. Here, success is about taking creative risks and facing our fears. It's about admitting that it won't look perfect and choosing to pivot when necessary.

You will do amazing things this year – even if it's your first time teaching remotely. For all the mistakes you make, you will have some amazing moments in which you know you are impacting lives.

If you had been on my driveway as those cars rolled by, it would have felt like a tickertape parade for a sports championship. Kids were screaming and cheering, and the teachers were waving and calling students out by name. Amid all the loneliness and isolation, the children in our neighborhood felt known and loved. Perhaps that's what matters the most in the end, and that's true whether you are on a video chat or in a physical classroom.

YOUR SHIFT
TO DISTANCE LEARNING
WILL BE FILLED WITH
UNCERTAINTY
AND, YES, QUITE A FEW
MISTAKES.
SO BE KIND TO YOURSELF
BECAUSE THIS IS HOW
YOU GROW.

CHAPTER 2

ANYTIME

ANYWHERE

LEARNING

We gather together for a lesson via video conference. After reviewing the norms, students engage in small-group discussions in their breakout rooms.

The lesson is going smoothly until . . . it isn't.

"What are the biggest challenges you face in classroom management?" I ask.

All at once, three students chime in, with each student saying, "You first . . . no you first," in an ongoing loop.

"I'm sorry. I meant to say this ahead of time. Use the chat function first to answer this question," I point out.

Students begin typing their questions in the chat and answering one another back and forth. I watch as four simultaneous conversations emerge as a few students struggle to track with the quick chat.

"I'm seeing some great ideas here, but I'd love for this to be a conversation. Let's go round-robin style, from left to right, and share our thoughts." However, after the first student shares her thoughts, the panel order changes on me. Suddenly, I'm frantically asking for students to raise their hands and volunteer. Eventually, I just go by the order on my class roster. After a rocky whole-class discussion, I shift to direct instruction.

"I'm seeing a trend here. Many of you are wondering what to do at the moment when a student is talking while you're talking."

I stand up and model how teachers can use volume, space proximity, and tone of voice as a preventative approach to classroom management. I ask students to mute themselves and practice their body language with me. They then practice their authoritative and approachable tone of voice. Several students struggle to hear a difference in my tone, given the delay in the video conference. Twice my screen freezes up. Several students get up for a restroom break. I don't blame them. This activity is a disaster. My pulse is pounding. I'm sweating. I can feel the lesson slipping away from me. So, I apologize and switch to a different activity.

I could blame the technology, but the truth is this was my fault. In the past, I practiced voice and space proximity with students in person, and it was always a huge success. But I had mistakenly attempted to substitute an in-person activity for a virtual video lesson. I failed to think intentionally about the nature of virtual communication, and everything fell apart on me.

That afternoon, I create a video showing space proximity and voice. I use a high-quality microphone and edit the video with a focus on clarity. Students then watch the video at home and create their own videos showing tone of voice and body language.

While this particular lesson failed miserably, our three additional class meetings go well. We have rich conversations in small groups and as a whole class. We use the chat function effectively and add polls, shared documents, and an annotated whiteboard to increase engagement. But it begins with rethinking the entire approach to my classroom-management course.

YOU CAN'T CONVERT COURSES

As you shift toward remote learning, you might be wondering, How do I convert my face-to-face course into an online course? The truth is, you can't convert a course. Learning isn't like a file that converts between a document and a PDF. We can't simply substitute new tools and do the same exact activity. In other words, that rich, spontaneous Socratic Seminar simply won't work in a discussion board or through a video-conferencing system. That amazing collaborative design challenge doesn't transfer easily when students move out of the makerspace and into their own homes. Instead, it will have to be re-imagined with new materials, new tasks, and new expectations.

When you focus on converting instruction, there is a tendency to see the limitations and miss the opportunities. You take a great in-person activity and then you try to do your best to substitute it with digital tools. But this will always lead to a deficit mindset in which you remain fixated on all the things you cannot do online that you were once able to do in person.

THE MINDSET SHIFT
FROM CONVERTING TO TRANSFORMING

What if we chose a different approach? What if we asked, "How do I transform my course?" rather than "How do I convert it?"

With transformation, you can leverage the creative and connective capacity of technology to design learning experiences that would have been inconceivable before.

This idea is at the heart of the SAMR Model.[1]

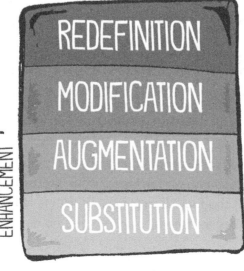

With the SAMR Model, the first two layers focus on using technology to enhance the learning process, while the next two layers focus on transforming the learning.

The first level, Substitution, uses technology as a direct substitution for the learning task with no significant change. So, a student who types an essay on the computer merely swaps a pencil for a keyboard. With Augmentation, the technology acts as a substitution with some augmentation. That paper essay moves to a Google Doc, where students can not only type and edit but also comment on one another's work. With Modification, technology enables significant task redesign. So, that essay is now a blog post. Students engage in online research, work collaboratively on a shared document, and publishing to an authentic audience. It is no longer an essay for a teacher. Instead, it is an article crafted for the world. With Redefinition, the technology allows for tasks that were previously inconceivable. That same essay becomes a multimedia package, with a blog post, a podcast, and a short video. The research, too, includes video conferences with experts and online surveys.

Note that redefinition isn't necessarily better. Sometimes, you simply need to substitute or modify a task with technology tools. However, the SAMR Model reminds us to think about the full capacity of technology to transform a learning task.

TRANSFORMATION IS ABOUT MORE THAN JUST TECHNOLOGY

When thinking about transforming a course, we need to think bigger than technology tools and ask ourselves, "What can my students do remotely that I cannot do in a physical classroom?"

With remote learning, we can take the learning process outside of the confines of the four classroom walls. Home learning allows us to build partnerships between school and home. We can find ways for students to learn within their own environments. They might engage in a scavenger hunt or a maker project using materials within their own environment. They can go out into nature to do scientific observations or to write poetry. At the K-12 level, students can interact with other students who are older or younger than them.

As a teacher, you can ask, "Where do I wish my class could go?" and then see if some of those places are free and open for your students.

We can also take differentiation to the next level. With remote learning, students can work at their own pace without being confined to a bell schedule or the tight pacing of a traditional classroom. Students can spend longer on assignments that take more of their time and speed through assignments they find easier. This is also an opportunity to empower them to own the time-management process.

ONE KEY QUESTION TO ASK IS, "WHAT ARE THE HIDDEN ADVANTAGES OF ANYTIME-ANYWHERE LEARNING?"

MODE OF LEARNING

Is it virtual? Online? Hybrid? Blended? Remote? The terms can seem a little confusing. Even educational technology experts disagree about the exact definition of each of these terms. However, for the purpose of this book, we will make these distinctions for the modes or contexts of learning:

- Remote learning (distance learning): learning that occurs away from the physical space of a classroom
- Virtual learning: using in-the-moment synchronous tools for learning
- Online learning: using asynchronous communication tools that are not bound by time
- Hybrid learning: a mix of in-person and remote learning
- Blended learning: Integrating technology and using online/digital tools within a physical, in-person space

Throughout this book, I will typically use the term remote learning for anytime-anywhere learning. However, I will also use the term distance learning. I will typically use the term virtual to mean synchronous learning and online to mean asynchronous. I recognize from a technical standpoint, virtual, online, and digital all essentially mean internet-based instruction. Let's take a deeper dive into definitions and examples of each of these terms. These distinctions are purely semantic.

THE 4 LEARNING ENVIRONMENTS

ONLINE	VIRTUAL	HYBRID	BLENDED
Online location often centered on an LMS	Online location often centered on a video conference	Physical classroom and online location simultaneous	Physical classroom with technology tools present
Tech-based	Tech-Based	Tech-Based and Tech-Integrated	Tech-integrated
Mostly asynchronous tools	Mostly synchronous tools	Synchronous and asynchronous tools	Mostly Synchronous Tools
Anytime? Yes	Anytime? No	Anytime? Maybe	Anytime? No
Anywhere? Yes	Anywhere? Yes	Anywhere? Maybe	Anywhere? No

ONLINE ←————————————————————→ **IN-PERSON**

You can think of these terms as existing on a continuum from online and asynchronous to in-person and fully synchronous

WHAT IS REMOTE LEARNING?

Remote learning is any kind of learning that happens away from the physical classroom. While it is often tech-based, remote learning does not require online or virtual technology.

ONLINE LEARNING
(ASYNCHRONOUS REMOTE LEARNING)

Asynchronous communication does not happen in real-time. Instead, it can happen over a longer period of time. Asynchronous communication might include a prerecorded video, an audio message, or an email. It also includes podcasts, videos, articles, and books. Most online course materials are typically asynchronous because of the ease of ability to read, view, or listen at one's own pace. In remote learning, instructors will often use asynchronous communication for direct instruction, as they introduce new ideas or concepts.

Students can easily re-watch a video or pause it to take additional notes. The following are the types of videos you might create:

- **Talking-head videos:** This term might conjure up images of the 1980s new-wave, art-funk band, but a talking-head video is simply a video in which the camera captures you speaking. In some cases, you might liven up a talking-head video with the use of slides or visuals. These videos work well for introductions, weekly updates, and inspirational messages to students.

- **Live-action videos:** A live-action video varies from a talking-head video in the fact that it captures an action or physical phenomenon. These videos might include slides and titles but also narration. Instructors might use live-action videos to demonstrate how to perform a particular physical action, including the staging in theater, a particular brush stroke in art, or a particular tool in science, technology, engineering, and math (STEM) or career and technical education (CTE) programs. Teachers might also use live-action videos to show a specific scientific process or a mathematical phenomenon.[2]
- **Screencast videos:** This type of video consists of a screen recording in which the narrator walks viewers through a specific action on a computer screen. A screencast video works well for technology tutorials and for any videos providing students with detailed instructions (such as how to create a blog). Screencast videos also work well as a way to go through student exemplars and explain specific features. An instructor might walk through features of a great essay in an English class or an example of a 3D model in an engineering class.
- **Annotated slideshow:** The instructor narrates a recorded PowerPoint or Keynote slideshow and records key information. You might embed specific videos within your slideshow to make it more dynamic. Afterward, simply export your annotated slideshow into a video format. Annotated slideshows work well as a replacement for a traditional lecture while you might need to teach specific concepts and offer an overview of the content.

In some cases, you may blend together elements of each video type and edit the videos using iMovie, Movie Maker, or any other video-editing software. For example, when I do onboarding videos at the start of a course, I blend together a talking-head video with screencast videos and then add slides from a presentation.

However, videos do not need to look polished and high-tech to communicate effectively. It's okay to have some "uhs" and "ums" and even a few mistakes. This can actually create an authentic feel and model risk-taking for students. Moreover, you don't need a fancy video studio to create high-quality course videos. You can use your smartphone, tablet, or computer.

Students can also use asynchronous tools for communication. When students create original content, they typically use asynchronous tools. This might be a sketchnote, a blog post, an infographic, a math problem, a video, or a podcast. However, they might still choose to use synchronous tools for elements of creative work, such as an audio interview with an expert, a synchronous video in solving a problem in engineering, or walkie-talkie app during an experiment. In collaborative work, students will often use asynchronous learning for research, inquiry, and project management but use synchronous tools for problem-solving and brainstorming. Furthermore, in performance-based courses, students can record themselves and compare it to a recording created by the teacher or professor.

Note that most of the time, your remote learning course will have elements of both online learning and virtual learning. You will likely have asynchronous prerecorded videos for how-to instructions and lectures. Afterward, you can use synchronous video or audio to discuss these ideas in a more interactive and dynamic way. You might also use a tool like an asynchronous video tool to have students create short videos that they post in a shared discussion area.[3] In terms of grouping, I have found that groups of three to four work best in synchronous video chats, groups of five to seven work well using walkie-talkie apps, and groups of eight to twelve work well with asynchronous video discussions or in an online forum. However, you'll likely need to navigate this through a process of trial and error.

VIRTUAL LEARNING
(SYNCHRONOUS REMOTE LEARNING)

Virtual learning is any type of remote learning that occurs synchronously. Synchronous communication happens in real-time, in the moment. This might be a video conference, a webinar, a live chat, or a phone call. It's essentially any of the type of communication you would do in person that you are now doing with digital tools.

Synchronous communication works well when you are planning for dynamic and interactive learning tasks. For example, you might want to use a virtual conference for guided practice on a discreet skill. A music, art, language, or physical education teacher might use a video conference for a quick performance assessment in which they can provide feedback in the moment. Synchronous learning also works well for small-group brainstorming, planning, and decision-making. In a larger group, virtual learning can help create a sense of community.

Virtual learning has its limitations, though. The synchronous, interactive nature makes it a challenge when students have unreliable internet or challenging schedules. It tends to grow less effective as groups increase in size. For this reason, virtual learning is not a great method for direct instruction or any time students are processing new information. It's also less effective in situations where you want to keep a permanent record of communication.

REMOTE LEARNING DOESN'T HAVE TO MEAN ON-SCREEN LEARNING

While we often think of remote learning as being virtual and online, we don't want to see students sitting down in front of a screen for eight hours a day. For this reason, it helps to design learning experiences that take students away from their screens. Working remotely should include physical, hands-on learning. It should incorporate movement and encourage students to interact with their world.

A teacher might design a maker project or STEM project with students engaging in rapid prototyping using items found around their environment. Another option might be a scavenger hunt in which students find items around their house to solve a problem. They might go on a nature walk and sketch their observations in a journal. Or, they might document elements of culture or history within their immediate neighborhood. Students might do physical exercise in their local environment. They might do sketchnoting to take notes and make sense out of ideas or use sticky notes for brainstorming.

Students don't need to choose a binary on-screen or off-screen approach. Many of these options involve a movement between the physical and virtual world. So, students might do a Genius Hour project and create something new.[4] However, they document their learning with a video or audio journal. They might even craft a how-to video or write a blog post. Students might do a hands-on maker project but then share their work to the class LMS or in a virtual class meeting. Many art teachers have had students recreate art masterpieces using physical items that they find around the house. While most of the work is done in person, students then document their process by snapping a picture with their smartphones.

It's also important that we remember the role of equity and access in taking things off-screen. Be cognizant of what materials students have and what resources they have access to. For example, if you're incorporating physical movement, some students might live in a large house and others in a crowded apartment. Some students might have a fully stocked craft room and others have a few limited supplies.

HYBRID
REMOTE AND IN PERSON

In the 1960's, cities throughout the United States built multipurpose stadiums for football games, baseball games, and concerts. These were supposed to be sleek, modern, and broad enough to encompass the needs of every entertainment industry. However, these stadiums weren't designed with the fans in mind, which led to have half-empty baseball games where fans had horrible sightlines. In football, athletes were losing traction on the baseball infield and slipping on the dirt. As for concerts, the stadiums were exciting but they lacked the sound quality of an auditorium or amphitheater.

This is the same challenge we are facing in hybrid learning. If we're not careful, we can all too easily design lessons that don't work for students at home or in the physical classroom. It can all too easily become a logistical nightmare as we attempt to be all things to all people.

I'm not a fan of teaching a hybrid lesson where half the students are at home and half the students are attending via video conference. On a purely functional level, it works. But it doesn't work well. It's the instructional version of a spork. By trying to merge together two incompatible formats, you're left designing lessons that lack the full range of options in either environment.

I made this mistake the first time I taught a pedagogy course where half of my students were in person and the other half were at home. I ended up lecturing in front of my computer camera so that students at home could see me via Zoom. I then faced my web camera at the board where students were expected to look at the slides. Fortunately, I had uploaded my slideshow to the LMS and students solved this problem. But still . . . it was bad.

When students asked questions in person, I would repeat it to the students on Zoom. When they had questions, I would repeat it aloud for the students in my face-to-face group. I attempted to place students at home with small groups who were in person, leading to bad echoes in the video chats. Eventually, I changed the grouping and modified the assignment. However, the lesson remained clunky and awkward.

I had created a spork.

However, hybrid learning doesn't have to be spork learning. I left that first evening with the realization that I had to change our entire hybrid model. I couldn't simply have students video conference in to the physical course and expect it to work. I had to find a new approach that would maximize the benefits of both face-to-face and virtual environments. That semester, I focused on the Differentiated Model. However, in other semesters, I have used the Multiple Tracks model and the Split A/B model.

The following are five different models for structuring hybrid learning. Every model has its own strengths and weaknesses. As educators, we need to be strategic about which model we select based on the needs of our students.

Model	Students at Home	Students In-Person
The Differentiated Model: Students at home and in-person engage synchronously on the same lesson.	Students use video conferencing technology to access the lessons.	Students meet in-person and often interact with students at home.
The Multi-track Model: Students work on the same lessons but they are divided into cohorts that exist in separate tracks.	Students at home can work asynchronously in an online track or synchronously in a virtual track.	Students in person engage in learning face-to-face without interacting with virtual and online groups.
The Split A/B Model: Students alternate days between being at-home and being in-person.	Students at home work on asynchronous assignments and do synchronous assignments in person.	Students in person make the most of face-to-face time by keeping things highly interactive.
The Virtual Accommodation Model: A small group of students join the in-person class.	Students participate in all of the same face-to-face activities using video conferencing.	Students participate in a typical face-to-face class with a liaison helping the virtual group.
The Independent Project Model: When a face-to-face lesson doesn't work off-line and only 1-4 students needs to work virtually, an independent project model works best	Students work independently on a project or an adaptive learning module. The process is fully personalized.	Students continue to work in their face-to-face environment.

1. THE DIFFERENTIATED MODEL

In this model, every student attends the class at the same time. However, you design differentiated activities for students who are at home and in person. It works well to make use of both synchronous and asynchronous communication tools for students at home and in person

Students begin by logging into a video conference platform from home or going to their seats in person. From there, you can differentiate your approach to the two different modalities (virtual and in-person).

Sample Class: Traditional Lesson

- **Warm-Up**: Students at home and in-person work on a warm-up that you have posted to your learning management system. You can set a timer in-person and online so that students know the time limits. This is often when you take attendance.
- **Direct instruction:** Students at home view a prerecorded flipped video by pressing play on the link you share in the video chat. Everyone in the video conference should be on mute. Meanwhile, you press play on the same video for your students in-person. This allows all students to access it together simultaneously.
- **Guided practice**: Students meet together as a whole class. They can submit their questions on a Google Form and you answer them, in the moment, in front of the computer so that students at home can hear. Or, you can allow students to use a wireless microphone and you can hook up the computer to speaker so that students at home can speak to the whole group class and also hear what the in-person class is saying.
- **Independent practice:** As students move into small groups to practice their learning, the students at home can work

collaboratively using the breakout rooms while students in person can meet in small groups. You can add accountability components by having students write in a shared document. At times, you might have student groups that include both in-person and at-home students but this is admittedly tricky.

- **Closure:** Every students fills out an online form for a closing activity.

Sample Class: Project-Based Lesson

- **Warm-up**: Students work on their blog posts
- **Direct instruction:** Students at home view a pre-recorded flipped video by pressing play on the link you share in the video chat.[5] Everyone, including the students, are on mute. Meanwhile, you can press play on the same video for your students in-person. This allows all students to access it together. This short video might be a quick review of the research process or it might be a key concept they need to learn connected to their project. This part is 5 minutes maximum.
- **Project time:** Students at home work on their projects with other students at home by being strategic with tech-based collaboration tools. Often, they start by reviewing their project progress on a spreadsheet or using a project management tool. From there, students use a mix of tools as they work on their projects. This is the bulk of the class time.
- **Closure**: Students reflect on their learning using an online form or they go back to their project management tool (project board, spreadsheet, calendar, etc.) to set project goals for the next day.

While this option keeps groups separated by learning environments or modalities (in-person or at home), students still interact with one another on the class learning management system. You can post questions as warm-ups in a way that creates a combined classroom community. You can also design assignments with mixed groups where students at home and in-person might work together for a smaller amount of time. They might give feedback using the 20-minute feedback system[6] or they could work on a shared document together in collaborative brainstorms. I love doing online carousel activities this way. Here, all students are in breakout rooms and every student has headphones. This helps prevent issues of echoes or bad audio quality.

2. THE MULTI-TRACK MODEL

This second model treats each group as an entirely different cohort within the same larger class. So, while students might learn the same lessons and the same objectives, they essentially function almost like separate classes. At the start of the course, students sign up for the virtual track (synchronous remote learning), the online track (asynchronous remote learning), or the face-to-face track. As you teach, you run the virtual and in-person lessons at the same time. Meanwhile, students in the online track can access the online modules on their own time. Here's what this looks like in practice.

Sample Class: Traditional Lesson

- **Warm-Up:** Students in all three tracks log in to their cohort's LMS and answer the same discussion question. You have the directions for logging in posted on the video chat for the Virtual Cohort and displayed on the board for the face-to-face group. Meanwhile, students in the Online Cohort post their answers on their own time.
- **Direct instruction:** Students at home in the Virtual Cohort view a pre-recorded flipped video by pressing play on the

link you share in the video chat. Meanwhile, you teach the same direct instruction in a more interactive way to the face-to-face group. Students in the Online Cohort watch the same flipped video as the Virtual Cohort. However, they simply need to watch and respond by the end of the day.

- **Guided practice:** You vary your guided practice depending on the day. So, you might do guided practice work with your in-person class while students in the Virtual Cohort engage in small group discussions to deepen their understanding of the content. The next day, you can reverse it and have the In-Person Cohort working independently or in small groups while you do direct instruction with the Virtual Cohort. Members of the Online Cohort have the option of joining the Virtual Cohort if they need additional guided practice.
- **Independent practice:** As students move into small groups to practice their learning, the students at home can work collaboratively using the breakout rooms while students in person can meet in small groups. Students in the Online Cohort can collaborate using asynchronous tools.

This second model is highly tailored to each learning environment. It has very few "spork moments." However, it is a real challenge in terms of prep work and logistics. For this reason, it sometimes helps to divide the cohorts into separate classes and allow different teachers to alternate teaching the virtual, online, or in-person groups.

For project-based learning, there's more flexibility. You can craft projects that allow the Online Cohort to work independently or to schedule collaborative project work time throughout the week. You can then do email and video conference check-ins. The Virtual Cohort can also work on the same projects and you can essentially place them in the breakout rooms immediately after they log in. Meanwhile, your face-to-face group can begin working on their projects the moment they walk through the door.

As the facilitator, you can move between groups in each location and help problem-solve and guide student reflection. When you need to do direct instruction, you can create a flipped video for students in the virtual or online environments and you can do the same type of direct instruction face-to-face when the moment arises.

3. THE SPLIT A/B MODEL

The previously mentioned models work best in situations where half the students are required to stay at home at all times. This is true in university courses where students live far away but it has also been true during the quarantine with families who do not want to send their students to a physical classroom building. However, in some cases, you might have all students opting in to face-to-face learning but you also need to maintain social distancing. Here's where the Split A/B model works well. A typical A/B Schedule might look like this:

- A Group meets Monday and Wednesday
- B Group meets Tuesday and Thursday
- Friday is for home room, study hall, and open office hours

With the A/B schedule, teachers can make the most out of face-to-face time by maximizing student interaction when they meet in the physical building. They can then have students watched flipped videos, do station rotations, engage in meaningful independent practice, or do independent projects when they are at home. In other words, the synchronous learning happens face-to-face and the asynchronous learning happens at home, when students can work at their own pace. Here are a few ways you might organize an A/B classroom:

- **Flipped Approach:** Students watch a video, read an article, or get a preview assignment that they do at home. Then, when they meet in person, they might do a lab to reinforce the ideas, engage in guided practice, or do small group intervention instruction. Teachers might even do shorter game-based learning activities or simulations to reinforce the concepts they learned at home.
- **Project-Based Approach:** There are a few options here. The first is to have students work on an independent project at home and a collaborative project in-person. This is the easier option logistically but it can lead to project fatigue. The second option is to have students work on their projects in person and then engage in more traditional work (watching direct instruction videos, doing skills practice work) at home. The third option is to have students work on their projects at home and at school. So, they might engage in inquiry in person and then do their research at home, where they convey their findings in a shared document. They can then meet in person to debrief the research and engage in ideation in person. From there, they might do prototyping in person and at home, using the same shared project management tools in class and at home. It's key that we keep equity in mind and that we allow students to bring home materials from the classroom when necessary.
- **Station Rotation Approach:** There many station rotation models you can use where you can rotate students through key skills and concepts in online and in-person groups.
- **Intervention and Enrichment Approach**: With this model, students engage in online learning and then show up to class with specific questions. Teachers then pull small groups for

intervention, clarify misunderstandings, and create options for meaningful enrichment activities. This isn't a study hall. Instead, it is a highly structured approach to maximize the dynamic, interactive elements of targeted help.

- **Seminar Approach:** This closely aligns with the college seminar model. Students do a reading, watch a video, or listen to a podcast. Then, when they are in person they engage in a Socratic Seminar. The whole focus is on maximizing group interaction time. So, students might do some reflective writing but the bulk of the class time is small group and whole class discussion. While the seminar model tends to be focused heavily on academics, teachers can also use it for social-emotional learning. It can be a time for community building.

4. THE VIRTUAL ACCOMMODATION MODEL

There are times when you have a small handful of students (figuratively, because, let's be honest, you can't fit your students in the palm of your hands unless you teach Smurfs) who need to work remotely while the rest of the class learns in person. In these moments, a virtual accommodation model works best. Here, you can teach the same lesson you would typically teach but have one student volunteer use the video chat and a single computer to allow students to participate. This person can sit near the teacher during direct instruction. You might still do a flipped video that the students at home watch. However, they might just watch you teach face-to-face. As they move into small groups, you can mute the video conference and let the students at home form a small group.

5. INDEPENDENT PROJECT MODEL

Sometimes your in-person activity simply doesn't connect with what students can do at home. It might involve a specific lab or a maker project. In these rare moments, you might need to do an independent project. Students can learn the same standards and focus on the same learning targets but they do so in a way that is separate from their classmates. One alternative is to do an independent project that students can do at home or in-person.

You might have students work on their own choice menus (an idea we'll explore later). Another variation might be a self-paced approach, where students have access to an adaptive learning platform where they can master the learning at their own pace. However, the independent project model is not ideal for most situations and it can lead to isolation and loneliness. Learning is inherently social, so the goal in this model should be to find ways for students to move into the other models instead.

THERE IS NO PERFECT MODEL

Each of these models work well in certain situations and poorly in other situations. As teachers, we can think strategically about how to design our learning so that we can optimize the benefits of each models. As schools, we can think creatively about when and how to use these models so that we avoid some of the pitfalls of a spork-based approach to learning. Even so, there will be mistakes. Learning is dynamic and complicated and hybrid learning adds another layer of complexity. But by being intentional, we can help students thrive in every learning environment.

BLENDED
TECH-INTEGRATED IN PERSON

The final approach is a blended-learning approach. This blends together physical learning and tech-based learning in a physical classroom. While many of the examples in this book can be easily adapted into blended environments, our focus will remain on remote and hybrid learning.

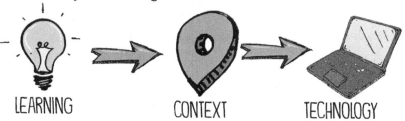

LEARNING   CONTEXT   TECHNOLOGY

START WITH THE LEARNING RATHER THAN THE TECHNOLOGY

As the teacher, you are the architect of your students' learning. You are the craftsperson designing new experiences. But there's no single right way to do it. Remote and hybrid learning will always be an experiment, and it varies depending on your subject, your context, and your students. Although the goal is transformation, it's important to begin with a focus on the learning rather than the technology. When you start with the technology, you run the risk of creating high-tech activities that fail to teach new concepts or skills.

Technology will grow obsolete. The tools you use today will likely be outdated in a decade. But those soft skills they develop will persist for an entire lifetime. So, as you plan for instruction, begin with core ideas of student learning outcomes, standards, or course goals you want students to master. Often, you will begin to envision a general concept of key projects or learning activities. But that's just the start.

After determining the student projects or learning tasks, you can think strategically about the mode of learning. Will your students be fully in person with a blended model? If so, you can easily choose high-tech and low-tech options. However, you will be limited by the constraints of the physical classroom. If you are going fully remote, you will likely have synchronous and asynchronous options. Students will have more flexibility with their schedule and their physical environment. Still, many traditional classroom activities will not be available. If you're going hybrid, you'll need to think through how to optimize activities to make the most use out of the in-person learning while also designing quality activities that make use of remote learning.

Once you've thought through the context or mode of the learning, you can then consider the technology you will use. The following categories are a few areas that you might consider:

- **Communication tools:** chats, video chats, social media, shared whiteboards
- **Creative tools:** podcasting, blogging, video production, image editing, Slideshows
- **Collaboration tools:** shared documents, shared sites, shared project-management tools
- **Mindtools:** concept mapping, spreadsheets, digital modeling, curation software

As you explore the available technology, consider the following questions:

- What do I want students to do? Think about the specific learning task and keep that in mind before selecting which technology tools or platforms to use.
- What hardware will students be using? In some classes, you might have students using tablets, such as iPads. In other classes, you might use laptops, including Chromebooks. This makes a difference for the apps you select and how they align with the learning tasks. A student can write a blog post on a laptop or a smartphone, but it will be easier on a laptop. They can record a video on a laptop, but the phone might work better for portability. Afterward, a laptop might make editing easier. Consider, too, how students might use multiple devices interchangeably and how those processes might work.
- Do these apps and platforms adhere to the policies? Here in the U.S., we have the Children's Internet Protection Act (CIPA)[7] and the Children's Online Privacy Protection Act (COPPA)[8] that dictate key information about student privacy. Some of the great tools that we might use in other industries are not compliant at the K-12 level. Take some time to research your local policies to make sure you are in compliance.
- What do these tools provide? Do an audit of the available tools and think intentionally about all the features they provide. It can be surprising how well certain apps work in different domains. For example, I had students use spreadsheets for project management. A spreadsheet might be old school, but it's a powerful tool for organizing complex data. Other students preferred to use a visual project-management software. It helps to limit your tools. Students can get overwhelmed when there are too many platforms with usernames, passwords, and class codes. Busy parents and guardians often struggle to manage all of these systems when they have multiple children at home. For this reason, you might want to coordinate with teachers in your building to decide on specific

common platforms. Similarly, if you are at a university level, you might do a survey to see which tools students are using and how you might pare it down so that it remains manageable for your college students.

- What is the cost? We expect technology to have a financial cost. However, technology can be time-consuming as well. This is especially true with some of the most robust and complex software. There's also a potential for a social or personal cost. I remember going full-force into technology and realizing that I wasn't asking students to speak face to face. I wasn't incorporating movement into my lessons. They worked collaboratively on screen, but they were missing the vital element of being present with their groups. So, I had to rethink the social cost of the technology and focus on incorporating some of the lo-fi, low-tech elements.

You'll make tons of mistakes as you shift toward remote and hybrid learning — and that's okay. The beauty is in learning from those mistakes and iterating toward better instruction. Seek out the experts in your own institution and be humble about what you don't know. Ask students for their input along the way. And over time, you'll develop some amazing distance learning lessons.

CHAPTER 3

HAVING AN
ADAPTABLE
APPROACH

YOU ARE NOT A
CONTENT-DELIVERY
MACHINE

We often use a metaphor of content delivery to describe the teaching and learning process. We use the phrase "deliver a lesson," and we ask, "Did the students get it?"[9] However, when we view learning through a content-delivery lens, we tend to focus on technology as we shift into remote and hybrid learning. We end up with adaptive learning programs that are little more than leveled worksheets. However, teachers know that learning isn't passive or even predictable. It's a dynamic, idiosyncratic process where students make sense out of new ideas in light of what they already know. It is inherently social and relational.

This is why, as an educator, you will always be more than a content-delivery machine. True, you design lessons and, yes, this requires you to find content. But this process is also relational. You are a curator finding new readings, podcasts, videos, and other course materials for students.

This curation begins with a deep knowledge of your subject area but also a relational knowledge of your students and an orientation toward justice. As a curator, you actively seek out resources that have true representation rather than mere tokenism. You engage in rich conversations with experts in culturally responsive and anti-racist teaching so that you can find materials that promote justice.[10]

You are also an architect who designs the structures and systems that facilitate learning. You design the framework for your courses, from the syllabus to the unit plans to the daily lessons. You choose strategies that maximize student engagement. However, this design process isn't cold or distant. As an educator, you're an artist, working on the craft of teaching. You're dreaming up new projects and lessons in a way that is often messy and can even feel confusing. You often feel your way through it. However, you're also a scientist, experimenting with new strategies and gathering data to see what works best in your immediate context. As you engage in these creative risks, you become an innovator seeking out the overlap between best practices and next practices.

You are a community builder. From day one, you are building relationships with students. It's often in the little things, like sending an email the first time a student misses a virtual class session. It's what happens when you give them opportunities to pursue their interests and chase their curiosity. As the community builder, you are empowering students to develop the shared classroom norms and procedures.

On a daily level, you set the tone with your approach to classroom management and in subtle things like the language you use and the sense of humor you bring to the community. Moreover, you help teams solve problems and resolve conflict during collaborative work. You find creative ways to develop trust and create a sense of presence even when students are working remotely.

In these moments, you are also a mentor. Students can feel relationally isolated in distance learning courses. However, when you provide meaningful feedback on student work, you are helping stu-dents reach their potential. When you check in on students with an email or when you engage in a one-on-one video conference, you are often listening and even providing guidance.

Notice that these aspects of your teacher identity are all relational. And these relational aspects are true whether you teach in person, remotely, or in a hybrid environment. In fact, these relational aspects might be even more important remotely, where the lack of physical space increases the necessity of relational engagement.

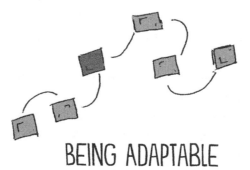

BEING ADAPTABLE

When shifting toward remote learning, you might feel like a brand-new teacher all over again. Suddenly, that amazing engineering project isn't possible without the high-tech makerspace you've been using. That thriving band program can no longer meet together to perform in the same room. You're amazing drama units don't work the same way without a stage or a theater. A class like physical education is no longer tied to a physical location. Those amazing Socratic Seminars[11] that you've refined over the years now might fall flat without the same body language and space proximity.

You grapple with how to make learning meaningful when your expertise has been developed in an environment where physicality was front and center. Typically, you have a strong sense of what strategies work best in your context. But with an entirely new context, there is a new learning curve with a new set of new mistakes you'll make along the way. This is why it helps to have an adaptive approach to hybrid and remote learning.

An adaptive approach involves starting small and being willing to move quickly when things don't work. While there is definitely intentional planning ahead of time, you are constantly asking, "How do I improve this?" This keeps you nimble as you iterate and improve.

An adaptive approach begins with an openness to new ideas. You're actively seeking out advice and looking for different approaches. As you shift toward virtual and hybrid teaching, you are re-imagining what the classroom will look like. You're asking big "What if?" questions that lead you to new strategies and approaches. But this doesn't mean you abandon what already works. Instead, you are looking for the vintage innovation overlap between best practices and next practices.

An adaptive approach treats each lesson as an experiment. Sometimes the lessons work and sometimes they fail. But even the failed experiments are opportunities to reflect and grow. This doesn't always feel good. It's frustrating when things aren't working – especially when you are already a master in the craft of teaching. However, as you adapt, you are able to recognize that you are gaining new skills as an educator. Note that an experiment isn't as simple as a binary success or failure. There are varying degrees of success that exist on a continuum. I'll be using examples from my own teaching experience with video conferencing.

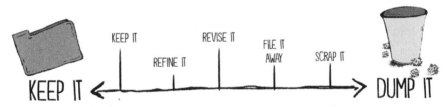

KEEP IT | KEEP IT | REFINE IT | REVISE IT | FILE IT AWAY | SCRAP IT | DUMP IT

- **Keep it:** This is the option in which you choose to keep the strategy and even use it again without changes. This is essentially the unicorn. No, it's even more rare than a unicorn. It's the rainbow-brindle unicorn. Super rare but also super magical. *Example: That SEL-related warmup was perfect for my video conference. I'm using it with my next class.*
- **Refine it:** Here, you choose to use the same strategy again with minor improvements. This is what we often do in face-to-face teaching. *Example: Small-group breakout rooms worked well, but I failed to put the question prompt where people could see it. I'll link that to a slideshow on our LMS next time so that they can see the question in their breakout rooms.*

- **Revise it:** With this option, you make significant changes to the strategy, lesson, or project. You might even choose to mash it up with another strategy to create something entirely new. *Example: In teaching classroom management, I should not have used a video conference to teach voice, space proximity, and body language. Next time, I'm doing a prerecorded video showing how this works and then I'll have students create their own videos. We can then debrief it with a video conference.*

- **File it away:** Sometimes, a strategy isn't a complete failure. It's just a failure in this particular moment. When this happens, you might file a strategy away for another time in another context. *Example: The video-conference scavenger hunt could still work at the secondary level but maybe not in the first synchronous video meeting that we have as a class. I think we need to clarify norms and expectations first and do some creative risk-taking. We might try a scavenger hunt with better instructions and a tie-in to the content in the middle of the semester. Maybe we'll add it to a maker project or even a virtual escape room.*

- **Scrap it:** This is a permanent delete option, where you realize that the project, lesson, or strategy was simply a really bad idea. *Example: Trying to have a free-flowing class discussion was a bad idea on a video conference. It turned into a lot of "you first . . . no, you first" interactions. It was awkward and just bad. It was really, really bad.*

You will have strategies that fit into each of these categories as you go through your remote-learning journey. Here's where humility is so critical. With an adaptive approach, you aren't tying your entire identity to the success of a lesson. You can admit that something was an epic fail without feeling like you are an epic failure as an educator.

In a trusted environment, this humility can extend into vulnerability. When you go to your students and admit that a strategy failed, you are modeling humility and creative risk-taking. You are letting them into your creative process and, at times, even asking for their feedback to help you refine your craft. However, this type of vulnerability requires mutual trust. There are some students who respond to vulnerability as an opportunity to manipulate an instructor and use their words against them. In a toxic environment full of distrust, vulnerability can be weaponized. Furthermore, there is an inherently higher cost to vulnerability for teachers of color who face institutional racism and implicit bias about their competency. In these cases, vulnerability can be risky. So, trust has to be a prerequisite for vulnerability. It's why it helps to focus the initial course activities on building relationships and developing trust.

DON'T DO IT ALONE

An adaptive approach also involves collaboration. The shift toward remote learning can feel lonely, but a trusted team can help you see that everyone is making mistakes and learning from failed experiments. This is why the iterative approach needs to extend into the larger school or university.

Adaptive teams are able to co-plan together in a way that builds on one another's strengths. The key here is delegation. We've all been on teams in which we have multiple meetings talking through various ideas, and you leave feeling like you have twice as much work as you would have had working alone.

By contrast, with mutual delegation, participants can have short meetings where they delegate tasks. They can then work independently. One teacher curates digital course materials while another teacher creates well-designed slideshows, and another teacher puts together the LMS and finds shared technology tools that the department or grade level will use together. Later, the team will regroup and provide mutual feedback and make revisions.

When collaborative teams embrace an adaptive approach, they invite feedback and openly exchange ideas. One of the things I love about my current department is how often small groups will meet together before the semester and do a writer's workshop for our courses. There's a certain level of vulnerability in saying, "Here is the course I created. Would you be willing to critique it?" This mutual critique has helped us grow into a more cohesive, tight-knit community. But it's also given us fresh ideas and helped us to learn from one another.

It's also important to reach out to the experts within your own community to get feedback on your course design. For example, you might not be much of a technology expert, but a district technology coach could provide you with a list of recommended apps to use. At the university level, you might have a dedicated technology or even an educational technology department. At every level, it helps to reach out to librarians, who can help curate resources and offer insights into how students can access information.

You might ask for special-education teachers or disability service personnel to review your course materials for advice on how to improve accessibility. Similarly, you could reach out to experts on language acquisition for strategies in how to ensure that English language learners (ELL) have access to necessary accommodations in online and virtual spaces.

Finally, you can reach out to the larger community. Invite parents and guardians to preview course materials and provide feedback. If possible, create a simple survey about their needs and wants from remote and hybrid learning. Ask students about their work and study habits. Once a course has launched, you can have students annotate the course and fill out surveys.

EMPOWERED TEACHERS EMPOWER STUDENTS

An adaptive approach requires institutional support. Educators need to feel the permission to make mistakes without being shamed or punished. They need to experience the freedom to experiment without being micromanaged. If we want educators to develop grit, their leaders need to give them slack. At the university level, this means taking into account a potential dip in student evaluation scores. At the K-12 level, this means expecting a potential decrease in student achievement scores. Furthermore, leaders can help by modeling vulnerability and trust so that educators feel the freedom to reach out to colleagues for help.

The permission to experiment cannot be a quiet permission, either. It's not enough for leaders to de-emphasize high-stakes accountability measures. Instead, they need to state clearly that they expect mistakes and failed experiments. These words must be backed by actions. When parents complain about a teacher's approach to virtual learning, principals need to defend teachers while also gathering feedback for improvement. Similarly, when students get frustrated with a professor who is new to virtual and hybrid teaching, the department chairs and deans need to defend their instructors and approach the situation as a chance to iterate and improve. It is critical that all stakeholders understand that the shift toward new modes of learning will include mistakes and missteps. Similarly, we, as educators, need to be humble about our own growth and remain open to feedback.

If institutions want to empower educators to take an adaptive approach, they will need to engage in systemic changes. For example, evaluations should include creative risk-taking and experimentation rather than merely student achievement. If possible, school policies should de-emphasize outcomes-oriented evaluations and instead focusing on continual improvement and creative risk-taking. Planning meetings need to include the freedom to pilot new projects and try new strategies rather than adopting a scripted online curriculum.

It's also important that educators give leaders the permission to make mistakes as well. Often, the shift to hybrid and distance learning involves navigating uncertain terrain. In the case of the pandemic, it has meant a rapidly changing social context with community members disagreeing sharply on when and how to re-open schools and universities. In some institutions, it has included a sudden increase in unemployment due to changes in enrollment numbers. Leaders are navigating new directives and policies at every level and these changes occur from day to day. There's no precedence for this.

I cannot begin to fathom the challenges educational leaders are facing right now as they try to change systems and launch new initiatives at a time when educators are rightfully scared and anxious. I have seen principals and superintendents tearfully describe the fear of staff members getting exposed to a deadly virus. That's a heavy weight on anyone's shoulders. I've seen deans and provosts who are facing sleepless nights as they face huge declines in enrollment that could lead to lay-offs. It's important that we allow our leaders to make mistakes and to iterate as they lead.

Ultimately, an adaptive approach requires a school culture that begins with a place of trust and humility. It means valuing transparency and vulnerability rather than high-stakes accountability. It involves giving the permission to have failed experiments and grow and improve as a result.

EMPOWERED TEACHERS EMPOWER STUDENTS

CHAPTER 4

THE CHALLENGE OF
STUDENT ENGAGEMENT

Student engagement can be a challenge in any classroom environment. You're constantly reading the room to see if students are committed and focused. You adjust the pace with attention to those slower moments when a lesson seems to drag on a bit. It's why you create moments for peer processing, use frequent transitions, and incorporate movement. You ask critical-thinking questions and seek out relevant resources. You use specific teaching strategies that increase buy-in and get students excited about the subject.

However, these student engagement strategies tend to be tied to the physical environment. As you shift toward hybrid and remote learning, peer engagement becomes more challenging and cumbersome. The use of asynchronous methods means you can't predict the pace of a lesson anymore. The lack of physicality makes movement more challenging. Meanwhile, your natural excitement and energy for your subject is harder to convey when students aren't physically present.

Teaching is an inherently physical job. But without an actual room, it's nearly impossible to "read the room." It's also challenging to get a sense of engagement in virtual meetings when everyone is in a different location with muted microphones.

Consider the role of distractions. In a physical classroom, you can use space proximity and body language to get a student's attention when they are distracted. But when students work from home, you can't redirect misbehavior. For students, it can feel as though class isn't actually in session. It becomes easier to miss a virtual meeting here and ignore an assignment there.

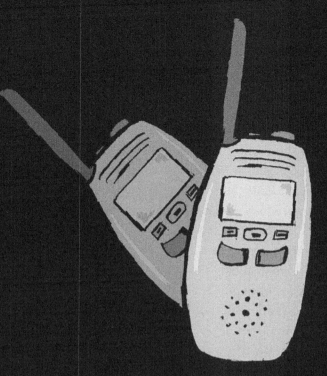

I KIND OF WANT TO GET A CHEAP
WALKIE-TALKIE AND RANDOMLY
INTERRUPT MY KIDS WHILE
THEY DO THEIR SCHOOL WORK
JUST TO GIVE IT THAT
AUTHENTIC FEEL OF AN INTERCOM
INTERRUPTING A CLASSROOM
7 TIMES AN HOUR

This is amplified by the sheer number of distractions in a remote environment. Often, the very tablets and computers they use for work are also their entertainment devices, so they can all too easily get sucked into binge-watching their favorite YouTuber or going through an entire season on streaming services. Even when they focus on their work, their smartphones buzz and ping with alerts for various games, messaging apps, and social media platforms. Many students have game systems designed to make gaming habitual, which means they can get lost for hours playing a game.[12]

Student engagement is a huge challenge in a culture of distraction, especially when those distractions occur at home. I recently created a student engagement survey of educators ranging from kindergarten to graduate school. It was fascinating to see that the biggest challenges were universal. Students were failing to turn in assignments on time. They weren't reading all of the directions. They attended virtual meetings, but they kept turning their microphones and video cameras off the whole time. Second-grade teachers and college professors alike made statements such as, "I feel like I am speaking to a wall," and "I just can't tell who is engaged."

In many cases, students aren't logging into the LMS, or they're logging in but not actually finishing the required assignments. The specific issues vary from class to class. It might be a matter of low attendance, low completion rates, or simply lower work quality than what students had done in person.[13] However, the larger challenge is something many teachers are experiencing — a decrease in student engagement compared to their former face-to-face instruction. This trend has been true everywhere. We've seen this in urban, suburban, and rural environments. These challenges exist in affluent and low-income schools, and they occur at every grade level in every subject area.

Student engagement is a major challenge for anyone teaching in virtual and hybrid settings.

I love how Philip Schlechty defined student engagement. "Engagement is active. It requires the students to be attentive as well as in attendance; it requires the students to be committed to the task and find some inherent value in what he or she is being asked to do. The engaged student not only does the task assigned but also does the task with enthusiasm and diligence."[14]

In 2002, Phillip Schlechty developed a framework for thinking about student engagement based on these two core ideas of engagement.[15] The first is attention. This is the idea that a student should be focused on the specific task without being distracted. The second is commitment. This is the idea that a student should find the task intrinsically motivating and challenging and, therefore, work toward mastering it.

At the bottom is rebellion, which involves diverted attention and no commitment to the task. This is the student who seems to be acting out and causing disruptions. As a result, they fail to learn from the task. In a physical classroom, a student in rebellion might be yelling out of turn, arguing with classmates, and throwing things. Though less frequent in remote learning, rebellion takes the form of cyberbullying or trolling. A student might leave abusive comments on another student's blog post or leave inappropriate and insulting comments in a discussion board in an attempt to get a rise out of classmates.

Next is retreatism, with no attention and low commitment. Unlike the rebellion, the student in retreat is not actively disrupting the learning but instead seems to be checked out. This student is often distracted and emotionally withdrawn from the task. As a result, this student learns little or nothing from the task. This is the most common lack of engagement in remote and hybrid learning. A student in retreat simply doesn't log in to the class LMS and doesn't show up to the virtual meeting. It often seems like apathy.

The next level is ritual compliance. This involves both low attention and low commitment. Unlike retreatism, a ritually compliant student isn't completely checked but instead is doing the bare minimum to avoid confrontation. This student will learn at a low level from the learning task and will not retain the information over time. In the spring of 2020, when many schools shifted to a pass/fail model for remote learning, the ritually compliant students would complete just enough work to earn a 60% in each class. They would choose the easier assignments and avoid anything too difficult. Frequently, they turned in work weeks after it was due, knowing they wouldn't face any penalties for late work.

Next is strategic compliance. Here, the student has high attention on the task but a low commitment. This student is playing the game of school, focused on things like grades, parental approval, rewards, or class rank. But the learning isn't intrinsically rewarding. As a result, this student will often perform at a high level but fail to retain the learning or transfer it to a new context. In many remote-learning courses, the strategically compliant student seems fully engaged but suddenly disengages when given an optional assignment. This is the student who sends five emails asking the instructor why an assignment hasn't been graded yet.

The final tier is engagement. This requires both high attention and high commitment. Here, a student will continue focusing even when the task gets more complex and challenging and often will choose to learn it even when it is ungraded. This student will learn it at a deep level and transfer it to new contexts. A fully engaged student works hard but also falls in love with the subject and the topics.

Both focus and commitment can be a challenge in remote-learning environments. Without physical space, it's harder to engage the class as a community. As teachers, we are missing those "aha moments" that happen with peak engagement. We can't monitor our students' attention in the moment. Many students are in a home environment where focus might be more of a challenge due to noise, chaos, and frequent distractions. The lack of physical space can make commitment a challenge as well, because the sheer number of other options can make learning seem less appealing.

This is why a focus on student engagement needs to first focus on the issues of access and equity. It can feel frustrating when students fail to turn in assignments or show up to class meetings. It's easy to assume students are being apathetic. However, as mentioned in chapter 1, some students are experiencing trauma and are struggling with basic functional tasks. I've seen a few of my own students (who are highly motivated and earning a degree in education) describe the "brain fog" and the sense of moving slowly through the day.[16] Furthermore, some K-12 students don't have the same access to technology. Some students are sharing devices with siblings or are in a Wi-Fi dead zone. Each home is different.

It's important that our default is to assume the best in our students and recognize that we don't always know the whole story. This is why we have to focus on equity before we focus on engagement. We'll be taking a deeper dive into equity in the next chapter. However, a lack of engagement can also be a lack of student ownership in the learning process.

EMPOWERING STUDENTS IN DISTANCE LEARNING ENVIRONMENTS

Many of these student engagement challenges are actually a lack of student self-direction. When a student fails to log into the LMS or show up to a meeting, that's a failure in self-direction. It might relate to executive function issues (which is why equity is key), but it can also be a failure to self-start. When a student fails to finish projects, it might not be a lack of interest. Instead, it might be a failure of self-management.

The students who are the best at navigating distance learning environments are not necessarily the most tech-savvy. Instead, they are the most self-directed.

In other words, these students have a sense of ownership over their learning. Yes, they are engaged, but they are also empowered. This empowerment can help fuel their engagement. By owning the learning, they have increased buy-in and thus better commitment. By self-managing, they are able to improve their focus. So, what does this look like? Here are a few ideas:

- Teach students to self-select the scaffolds. The idea is to teach students how to find specific learning supports that are universally accessible to your entire class. You might design scaffolds for language, including front-loaded vocabulary or sentence stems. You might also provide tutorials for academic concepts and create graphic organizers that all students can access. You might also curate a set of technology tutorials that students can access at any time. The goal is to empower students to be self-directed when they face challenges, so that they say, "I know where to go for help and I know what to do."
- Create opportunities for ownership in virtual meetings. Find specific ways to increase student feedback and interactions in virtual class meetings. Design activities that tap into their curiosity and creativity and even allow students to use items from their physical environment.
- Provide choice and flexibility in online assignments. A simple choice menu is often one of the best ways to introduce student voice and choice in a structured way. In a future chapter, I'll be sharing four different ways to use choice menus to pro-vide flexibility and choice in your online assignments.

64

- Tap into student interests. When students own the learning, they get an opportunity to pursue their own interests and passions. This varies by subject and grade level, but the goal is to empower students to pursue their interests and passions within the class setting.
- Empower students to own the inquiry process. Students should have frequent opportunities to ask clarifying questions to make sense out of confusing content. They should ask one another diagnostic questions as they engage in problem-solving. They should ask critical-thinking questions as they engage in deep dialogue. But they also need a chance to do research, gather data, and share their answers with an audience.
- Empower students to own the creative process. At some point, distance learning should include creative work. This might involve a design sprint or divergent thinking activity. Or, it might be a larger project-based learning (PBL) unit. Regardless of the approach, students should own the entire creative process.
- Empower students with collaborative learning. Remote learning doesn't have to mean working alone. Using both synchronous and asynchronous tools, students can own their learning through meaningful peer collaboration. The key is to design distance learning tasks that use both structure and interdependency and help students self-select their synchronous and asynchronous communication tools.
- Empower students to own the assessment process. In order to improve, students need meaningful feedback. They need to set goals and reflect on their progress. For this reason, it's important that we craft self-assessments and peer assessments that can boost metacognition and help students determine where they are and what they will do next. This is especially critical in a distance learning environment, where teachers

won't always be physically present to provide formative feedback.

A GRADUAL RELEASE APPROACH

Student ownership is not as simple as merely letting go of control as an educator. To empower students, we need to design our courses with specific structures that help facilitate ownership. This requires intentionality on our part. In the upcoming chapters, we'll explore specific strategies for building self-direction in key areas of student learning.

Even so, some students may struggle with the freedom they experience when they first own their learning. It can feel overwhelming. This is especially true at the university level, where students have spent years in largely compliant environments following the rules and doing what their teachers ask.

It can help to take a gradual release of responsibility (GRR) approach to student ownership.[17] You might start out with course documents that allow students to self-select scaffolds. But in this phase, you might still need to teach exceptional learners how to use specific accommodations. Over time, they will self-select what they need. You might also begin with a choice menu at first and then move on to a project where students can own the creative process. Slowly, you introduce more student ownership into collaborative work and you pilot some small self-assessments and peer assessments.

Ultimately, student ownership is about more than just increased engagement or deeper learning. Empowered learners develop the soft skills needed to thrive as lifelong learners and to become the makers and problem-solvers we know they can be.

CHAPTER 5

PROMOTING EQUITY
IN DISTANCE LEARNING

About a decade ago, a group of eighth-grade students gathered in front of my classroom at 6:00 a.m. Although we lived in a desert climate, they shivered in the cold winter air.

"Can we work inside?" a boy asked.

"I'm fine with this but you're really not supposed to be on campus right now," I said nervously. School wouldn't start for another two and a half hours, and I wasn't sure how our new principal would feel about me violating school policy. Then again, I couldn't just send them home.

They plugged their laptops into their chargers and continued to work on their shared document.

Finally, one of them said, "Hey, Mr. Spencer, you got us into trouble last night."

"I got you in trouble?" I asked.

"Yeah, you got us in trouble. Or, almost in trouble," a girl pointed out.

"I have no idea what you're talking about," I responded.

"They said we were littering," a boy said.

"Loitering," his group member corrected.

"You were the one who told us they had free Wi-Fi, but they don't actually want you to use it. We were paying, customers, too."

From there, they explained how they had met as a group to work on their project. But one member no longer had internet at home, and the other two members lived at the trailer park a block away, which is essentially a Wi-Fi dead zone. So, they walked a hundred yards to an apartment complex with lightning-fast internet. They met up with another student in their class who let them work on their project. However, they had to leave at dinnertime, so they went to a fast-food place, where they each bought a drink and kept getting free refills as they worked for hours on their project. A few hours later, one of the workers asked them to leave, so they kept working outside by the front door. The worker then threatened to call the police for loitering. So, they decided to meet at school early in the morning to work on their project.

As they explained the whole story, I was struck by the sheer problem-solving involved. They had worked within tight constraints and connected with other classmates all with the hopes of finishing a project on time. However, when I dug deeper into the issue, I found that they were moving slower on the project because I had failed to provide necessary language supports and academic help. I had provided scaffolds in person, but I hadn't incorporated them into our LMS. Moreover, there were small technology skills I had assumed they knew that had tripped them up. For example, they assumed each student could edit a blog post simultaneously in a way that resembled a Google Document. So, they lost huge chunks of text when one of them pressed the publish button. Although the assignment was built on student voice and choice, I had failed to address critical elements of equity and access.

This moment was a reminder that lack of engagement is not necessarily a lack of student motivation. Often, students are excited about a particular lesson or project, but they face steep challenges and systemic barriers in their remote-learning experience. Sometimes it's an issue of internet access or technology hardware but it might also include systemic racism and white privilege within the structures and content of the school system. It might involve a lack of access to the academic language, to key accommodations, and to the technology needed to thrive in a remote or hybrid learning environment.

EQUITY IN DISTANCE LEARNING

If we want to empower students in distance learning, we need to focus first on access and equity. This begins by ensuring every student has equitable access to technology. Not every student has the same device or the same internet connection. This is why it's critical to work with all stakeholders to provide increased access to technology. At a schoolwide level, you might provide a laptop checkout system and additional Wi-Fi hot spots.[18] But access to technology is not enough to guarantee access to remote learning.

Students also need access to additional academic supports. Some of your students might not be native English speakers and, as a result, they need access to sentence stems, visuals, front-loaded vocabulary and other accommodations that you provide in person.

Furthermore, exceptional learners need accommodations and supports in distance learning. As a teacher, you might want to re-read the individualized education plans (IEPs) and any of the 504 plans to provide necessary accommodations.[19] If you're in a K-12 environment, lean in to the special education teachers and disability support staff to think through how you will make your instruction universally accessible. If you are at a university, you might also have access to disability support services. But equity goes deeper than merely access to educational opportunities. As educators, we need to promote equitable practices in the systems we design and the materials we use.

It's easy to step into digital spaces and forget that they are not socially neutral. However, the systems that perpetuate injustice offline exist online as well. Pay close attention to the role of gender and race in your online instruction. There's a tendency for people to assume a false social neutrality online, but you need to address power dynamics. It helps to find experts in Culturally Responsive Pedagogy and ask them for a critique of your online materials so that you can find areas where you need to improve. We must also focus on instructional strategies that promote anti-racism in our teaching practice.

I readily admit that I am on this learning journey of anti-racism. I still have implicit bias and commit microaggressions as an instructor. It continues to be a journey in which I make mistakes. I do not pretend to be an expert on race or equity. However, there are many great resources, including books, courses, social media chats, and conferences that focus on equity and anti-racism.[20]

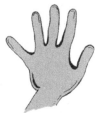

ENSURING ALL STUDENTS HAVE ACCESS TO LEARNING OPPORTUNITIES

Student empowerment begins with universal access. Every student needs to have access to the content, to the knowledge, to the tools, to the strategies, to the teacher, and to the classroom community. We can't always guarantee that students are going to have an equitable experience. Even when we actively work toward equity, injustices will still remain. However, there are strategic things that we can do to try to level the playing field and provide access to students as much as possible.

ACCESS TO TECHNOLOGY

The first area to consider is access to hardware. This is the idea of making sure that students have access to the specific devices that they need. Some districts have a bring your own device (BYOD), where students might be using devices that they have at home. However, not everyone has one-to-one devices at home.[21] In addition, not every device is the same. One student might have a decade-old laptop while another student has a brand-new Mac-Book Pro. Some students are using laptops, others tablets, and others smartphones. For this reason, your institution might need to run a checkout system, where students can borrow the same type of laptop or tablet that they use at school.

It's also important to remember that some students do not have access to reliable internet access. In certain rural areas, Wi-Fi speeds can be prohibitively slow, making video conferences impossible. In some cases, school districts have provided Wi-Fi hot spots by parking internet-enabled buses in certain neighborhoods. Universities have provided students with mobile hotspots. But, inevitably, we cannot assume that all students will have access to the internet at all times.

This is why it's important to use both synchronous and asynchronous communication. When doing a virtual class meeting, you might allow certain students to text key points to the teacher, and you can video record the meeting for replay later on. When providing tutorials, you might include text-based tutorials with .gifs that function as simple animations for students who can't access the video instructions. It also means that you are using tools that still allow them to feel a sense of participation. You might have students annotate a shared document according to their own schedule or participate in an ongoing asynchronous chat. You can allow students to select from articles, podcasts, and videos in a way that fits their schedule, their devices, and their internet.

Whenever possible, provide learning activities that students can access on multiple devices. Maybe they can't join the video conference easily, but they can listen to an audio podcast on a smartphone, tablet, or laptop. Similarly, students can collaborate using productivity tools that are device agnostic. This allows each student to participate without having to be tied to one particular type of hardware.

ACCESS TO TECH KNOWLEDGE

Having access to the technology is great, but it doesn't guarantee that every student will be able to use it. Some students will struggle with certain basic technology skills, even if they have technology hardware and software. For all the talk of students being "digital natives," some students struggle with uploading an assignment to an LMS or leaving a comment in a shared document.[22] Many students have used their personal devices for entertainment purposes, like watching viral videos or playing games. They aren't digital natives. They're consumer natives.

As teachers, we can improve this by creating a technology onboarding for students. They might have a checklist with links to tutorials for how to do certain tasks. Or you might form a technology help team of students who would be willing to talk over the phone or video conference with students who are learning the technology for the first time.

You might conduct a student survey of technology skills. Start out by making a list of every technology platform you plan to use and then breaking down the specific, discreet skills they need. For example, in the case of a shared document, can they create a new document? Can they share it with a classmate? Do they know the differences in the layers of privacy? Can they insert a comment? Can they highlight text? You can continually revise this survey as you notice other technology skills that students might be missing.

It also helps to have a curation of technology tutorials demonstrating how to create slideshows, edit videos, make podcasts, post blog posts, or navigate the LMS. You might be feeling overwhelmed at the prospect of creating all of these videos. However, there are so many content creators who have already created quality tutorials. If you think about the apps or programs that you use, most companies have onboarding videos but they also have tutorials.

Instead of trying to create all these tutorials yourself, you can curate these tutorials and help students access technology skills. You can then empower students to find the technology help when they have questions. Instead of stepping in and helping students every step of the way, you might say, "I need you to find the appropriate tutorial and watch the video." If possible, see if you can partner with grade-level teammates, technology specialists, librarians, or teachers in your department to create a single shared curation of resources. This way, students have a common document that they can access in any class. At the university, you might have a dedicated technology team as well as librarians who have put together specific tutorials. There's a good chance that they have already created a set of technology tutorials students can access.

At times, though, students will need additional technology help. In these moments, a student technology team can be helpful. Here, students can submit a help ticket or send an email to the student tech team, who then uses video conferencing (or in some cases, a phone call) to help problem-solve key technology issues.

This can free up the teacher's time while allowing a small tech help team to learn to problem-solve, communicate, and show empathy toward others. Note that you will need to provide some training upfront for your technology team. You might need to model a few scenarios with them. But the early investment in time can pay off later.

ACCESS TO ACADEMIC SUPPORTS

Students also need access to academic supports. Every exceptional learner needs access to accommodations. In the U.S., this means being cognizant of Americans with Disabilities Act (ADA)[23] and the Individuals with Disabilities Education Act (IDEA)[24] requirements. You will need to follow the specific legally binding accommodations of IEPs and 504 plans. You might need to connect with district personnel to find assistive technology.

While the accommodations will vary even more with special-education students (and you should always check the IEP), here are some examples:

- providing additional handouts to facilitate task-analysis and executive function
- pulling small groups for additional interventions
- conducting additional one-on-one check-ins with students and their parents or guardians via phone calls or video chats
- sending slideshows and materials to students ahead of time before video conferences
- creating outlines with bulleted points to keep students focused
- providing the necessary assistive technology

- teaching special-education students how to access necessary tools and tutorials
- being flexible with deadlines and requirements around specific tasks

It's important that you meet, as a team, to work with special-education teachers to determine what accommodations will look like when moving to remote and hybrid learning. If possible, you might contact each special education student's parents or guardians to review accommodations and go over expectations for the remote learning experience. This is an opportunity to empower exceptional learners to be their own advocates. By listening to them and demonstrating empathy, we honor their agency as learners. Similarly, if you work at a university, you might schedule a meeting with individual students and disability services to craft a plan for your class.

It can help to meet with special-education experts to go over specific course design elements. For example, the use of emojis, tables, and certain graphics can work against the voice-to-text software.[25] Certain color schemes can be a challenge for certain students with autism.[26]

We can empower all students to be self-directed by self-selecting scaffolds in their own learning. Every student should be able to access tutorials, graphic organizers, and tools to access academic content. In other words, provide as many scaffolds as possible for all of your students and let them determine what's appropriate.

For example, if a student is struggling with linear equations, they might need a video tutorial, walking them through the process of finding an equation by looking at a graph. However, an honor's algebra student might watch the same video as a quick refresher while doing a more complex algebra problem. You might have a "how to revise an essay" anchor chart and checklist that you have used in a small group with special-education students. However, other students might review the anchor chart when they are editing. You might have a student who is hearing impaired and needs closed captioning, but all students can choose to turn captioning on to reinforce what they hear in a video. Or, you might have image descriptions designed for visually impaired students, but then you find that other students can benefit from the ability to hover over a picture and get a text-based description.

This is at the heart of the universal design for learning. By designing courses that are universally accessible, every student can actually benefit as a result. By empowering students to self-select those scaffolds, you actually end up having a more inclusive environment that is more accessible for students.

ACCESS TO LANGUAGE SUPPORTS

Academic supports might include tutorials, scaffolds, and graphic organizers for all students. However, sometimes the deeper issue is that of language. For example, students might struggle with a video conference because it is moving quickly without think time and the instructor is not using visuals or providing access to sentence frames or clozes. While the accommodations vary depending on language levels, some common ELL and ESOL accommodations might be as follows:[27]

- front-loading vocabulary
- providing additional think time within group projects so that ELL students can process information
- providing translating help or partnering them with someone who is multilingual
- incorporating resources in their first language

- providing leveled sentence stems to help with discussions and writing
- providing mini-lessons on verb-tense structures or providing verb-tense formulas for complex texts within a project
- using visuals within the project to help facilitate language development
- incorporating technology tools, such as the option to slow down videos or audio during the research components of a project (the x .5 or x .25)
- paying attention to a students' affective filter and finding ways to reduce fear and anxiety they might experience during a project

Notice, again, that when you make these language supports universally accessible, you allow all students the opportunity to improve their language and discourse.

START WITH EMPATHY

At the basic level, we need to think about digital access. Not every student has the same access to technology. But we also need to go deeper than technology access and view equity through the lens of empathy. It's important to remember that not every student has the same access to a quiet workspace at home. Not every student has the same access to physical materials. Often, courses switch to distance learning because of a catastrophic event, like a natural disaster or, more recently, a pandemic. So, some middle-school students are babysitting siblings because their parents are essential workers, and others are living in a state of uncertainty with parents who have been recently laid off. At the university level, students might be working multiple jobs while managing a family in crises and dealing with the loss of a loved one.

In these moments, students at every level are likely to be experiencing varying degrees of trauma and post-traumatic stress disorder (PTSD).[28] These catastrophic situations can exacerbate mental-health issues.

As educators, we need to take the time to discover the whole story. It's easy to view disengagement as apathy or laziness, but a student might miss an assignment because the internet is spotty or they are facing increased stress at home. A student might fail to log in and check assignments because they are experiencing severe depression and anxiety.

An empathetic approach means taking the initiative to reach out when students miss a virtual meeting or haven't logged in to an LMS. I've been amazed by all of the teachers who have made phone calls to parents and guardians to see how they are doing. Together, all stakeholders can design a plan to make distance learning work.

An empathetic approach might include flexibility with deadlines and missed work. Allow students to resubmit work if need be. Let them turn work in later. Some would say this approach models low expectations, but I think this approach actually models higher expectations because you're saying, "I'm going to let you turn this in late, but my expectation is that we can find a way for you to get this done. I'm not going to let you get away with failing. I'm going to be right beside you, supporting you."

We can't ensure full equity and access for students. There are injustices outside of our control as educators. However, we can provide scaffolds and supports that help students increase their access to the learning. We can do this in a way that honors student dignity and centers on student agency. When this happens, we can start focusing on how to build an empowered community.

CHAPTER 6

BUILDING AN EMPOWERED COMMUNITY

During the pandemic, many students described feeling lonely and isolated as they shifted into online environments. This disconnect is amplified when online courses are designed with only individual work in mind. Over two decades ago, researchers Anderson and Garrison demonstrated that success in an online course depended on the relationship between the student and the content, the student and the instructor, and the student and classmates.[29] When students fail to connect with their instructor or with their classmates, they disengage.

This disengagement results in lower attendance, lower assignment completion, and lower achievement. In other words, by every metric imaginable, students learn less and perform worse when they aren't connecting with others. On a more human level, students need to connect relationally to their classmates and their teacher. They need to feel a sense of belonging. They need to be known and respected.

Teaching is deeply relational in any learning environment, but relationships are more important than ever in remote-learning courses. As educators, we need to build community in a way that honors student agency. It starts by getting to know students. Throughout this book, we will explore these ideas in-depth, but here are a few ways you can get to know students.

- **Surveys:** There are so many different options for student surveys. You might do an interest inventory, where they rate their interest in certain topics you will cover in class. They might share ideas of topics they like, novels they've read, TV shows they watch, video games they play, or music they listen to. You might ask students about communication preferences. How often do they want you to email them and do a check-in? Do they prefer videos or text-based instructions? In some cases, you might ask questions about their workspace or technology to help provide additional resources. While the survey is a one-on-one form of communication, you can create spaces where students share their interests with their peers. Each student shares their anthem, a song that feels nostalgic, and a song that people would be surprised that they enjoy. You can then create a Spotify playlist that students can access if they want to explore new music. See the next page for the prompt.

- **Show and tell activities:** We'll explore this idea in-depth in a future chapter. However, show and tell can be an opportunity to choose a specific item and explain why it matters to them. It could be an item that represents their hobbies or interests, but it might also be an item that represents their culture.

- **Maker projects:** When students do a maker project, we get a snapshot of their creative process. This can be a powerful way to help them find their creative voice.

- **Geek-out activities:** we can focus on specific ways that students can share their geek interests with their classmates. It might be a Geek Out Blog or a Genius Hour project, but the goal is for them to share their passions and interests with the larger community.

WHAT IS YOUR
MIX TAPE?

#1: NAME THE SONG THAT REPRESENTS YOUR ANTHEM

#2: NAME THE SONG THAT MAKES YOU FEEL NOSTALGIC

#3: NAME THE SONG THAT PEOPLE WOULD BE SURPRISED TO KNOW YOU LISTEN TO

BUILDING AN EMPOWERED COMMUNITY

Collectively, we can honor student agency by bringing students into the planning and decision-making process. One way to do this is with optional virtual student leadership teams. Think of it as a planning session with your students rather than your colleagues. The process is entirely democratic. Here's a sample agenda:

Agenda

- Quick individual check-in: Each student says one high, one low, and one random fact about themselves.
- Open feedback on what is going well in the course: You might ask specific questions about policies, practices, or lessons. For example, "What is going well with student collaboration?" or "What was your favorite mini-project?" Or, you can keep it open-ended with a question like, "What has been your favorite part of the course so far?"
- Open feedback on what could be improved: Again, this might be specific, with a question like, "How can we improve the course design?" or "What would you have changed about our last virtual meeting?"
- Share ideas: In this phase, each group member shares an idea of something they would like the class to do. To avoid judgment, you might just solicit ideas without getting feedback.
- Ask for feedback on an idea: Here, you might share an idea of something you would like to try with your students. It might be a project or a unit plan. Or, it might be a strategy or a new policy.

- Decision-making: This is optional, but you might want to make some decisions collectively as a group.
- Summarize and clarify: In this last phase, you summarize key ideas and allow for any clarifications that might be necessary.

The student leadership team is a small example of boosting student ownership in the classroom community. Another option is to do student surveys in which you ask the entire group for feedback and solicit new ideas. Toward the beginning of the year, you can also negotiate norms. You can also work together to come up with classroom procedures and systems. The goal is for students to feel they have a voice in the classroom community.

Another option is to provide students with specific classroom jobs or responsibilities. In a physical classroom, students might collect papers, organize supplies, or take care of the calendar. In an online or virtual space, students might volunteer to be a tech geek (helping students problem-solve issues), classroom reporter (sharing the class learning journey with parents or guardians), quality assurance manager (double-checking the course calendar and assignments), or any other job that students can own.

Student ownership also includes honoring students' cultural assets. This is why it's important to embrace culturally responsive teaching practices. If you haven't already, you might take some time to explore Geneva Gay's work on Culturally Responsive Pedagogy and consider how this might apply to an online and hybrid setting. Cultural responsiveness extends to everything from making sure there is diverse representation in course materials to having a positive view of a students' abilities. Gay also identifies choice and authenticity as an element of culturally responsive teaching.[30] It's important that students have a space in the community where they can share their expertise and tap into their interests. As Gay points out, students should be "personally involved in their education."[31]

VOICE AND CHOICE
BEGIN WITH HAVING
A VOICE IN YOUR
OWN COMMUNITY

A culturally responsive class affirms student identity, which, in turn, can help create a sense of ownership of the classroom community. It also solidifies a set of shared values. You can make these values explicit by asking students individually and collectively, "What values do you want our community to have?" From there, as trends emerge, you can name these values and engage in hard conversations about the extent to which your teaching practices align with these values.

While it's important to engage in hard conversations, it's equally important to embrace a culture of joy, fun, and even frivolity. Dean Shareski is a master educator who has taught for decades in in-person, online, and hybrid environments. In a brilliant TEDx Talk, he posed the question, "Whatever happened to joy?"[32] In it, he explored how high-stakes accountability measures had begun to rob classrooms of joy and how subversive teachers had actively cultivated joy, not as a means to better learning, but as an end in itself. While I agree that joy should be an end rather than merely a means to an end, we know that joy can impact a student's affective filter and increase motivation. Joyful environments can help facilitate community and build relationships. Moreover, humor can actually model creative risk-taking. After all, every act of humor is a small risk. There's always the chance that humor will fall flat, and you'll feel embarrassed.

When I taught middle school, we had a wordplay wall at the back with ridiculously bad dad jokes (things like "fire drill" and "curriculum knight" and "graduated cylinder"). We had Easter eggs hidden throughout the classroom. We had our own version of a Rick Roll. If someone asked you to "share a link," you had to "Cher a link" instead, sending them to a music video from Cher. One year, I put wheels on a drink coaster and called it our roller coaster. Students would tell their younger siblings that our class had a roller coaster and on student conferences, they would say things like, "You can't find the roller coaster? It's here. Keep look-ing."

These goofy jokes helped create a cohesive classroom commu-nity. Students would add silly dad jokes to the word wall in the back. In a small way, humor helped lead to student empowerment. Humor and fun can help define a positive classroom culture. This is especially true in online and virtual spaces, where inside jokes and goofy traditions can make the space feel more human. If you don't feel particularly creative in your sense of humor, you might ask stu-dents to submit jokes or memes via email. You can then vet the submissions and create a "joke of the day" on your LMS or in daily emails. This might seem superfluous but this sense of levity and joy can be empowering for your students.

Community building is also structural. Although you are inter-acting in a relational way, you are also the architect designing spaces where students can interact and collaborate. Students often disengage from the community when courses feel disorganized and confusing, even if they enjoy the instructor and their class-mates. It helps to provide a consistent schedule and consistent design for assignments and projects. One student put it this way, "I want to know my classmates but I also want to know what I'm doing. My favorite online teachers are the ones who give us a road map for where the course is going."

THE POWER OF STUDENT CHECK-INS

Students need to feel known and heard at an individual level as well. One simple way is to do a social-emotional pulse check as a warm-up in virtual meetings. For example, when students were facing the first week of a quarantine, I asked them to create their band name by combining the name of their snack food they had been eating and how they were feeling.

This created a sense of humor and levity, but it also sent the message that it's okay to not feel okay at the moment. It's okay to be wearing sweatpants. And, while I prefaced it with the importance of making healthy eating choices, it was a recognition that we were all struggling on some level. When students then met in small groups, they were able to share their feelings more openly.

It was a reminder that distance learning doesn't mean we have to be distant. As teachers, we can be intentional about creating a sense of presence with our students. This begins by doing frequent check-ins. These check-ins might focus on social-emotional elements, such as wellness, emotional status, and social connectedness. This type of check-in can be as simple as a "How are you doing right now?" or "How are you doing with distance learning?" It might even begin with a short conversation about a student's life, such as, "How is dance going for you?" or "What video games are you into?" These little questions can send the message that you care about your students and you want to know how they are doing. Other times, it might be a more in-depth check-in with a student, a caretaker, and the school counselor or psychologist.

Other times, the check-in might have a more academic focus. You might ask students questions about their hybrid learning experiences, including how they are navigating their courses, how they are managing their time, and how they are handling the work-load. This is often when you address issues of late work or a lack of engagement. In these moments, it's important to listen first and then help students develop a plan of action. In some cases, you might ask students about the social elements of school, including how they are getting along with their group members or how well connected they feel to the classroom community.

These academic check-ins might relate more closely to the class assignments and projects. You might provide some targeted help for students who are struggling. You might need to clarify mis-conceptions and provide students with additional resources or scaffolds. You might also help students set and track specific aca-demic goals.

We can conceptualize these check-ins on a continuum with the social-emotional check-ins on the more personal side and the tar-geted tutoring on the more academic side.

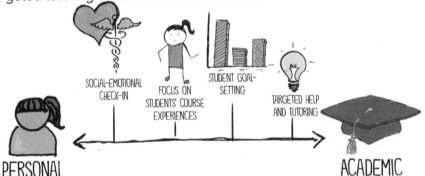

SOCIAL-EMOTIONAL CHECK-IN

FOCUS ON STUDENTS' COURSE EXPERIENCES

STUDENT GOAL-SETTING

TARGETED HELP AND TUTORING

PERSONAL

ACADEMIC

In general, teachers tend to focus on the personal elements first and move toward the more academic approach later. How-ever, some students are doing well emotionally and really want a check-in to be academically focused. It's why there's no single right way to approach this. In some cases, a conversation begins on an academic level and then shifts toward a more social-emotional side as students share how they're actually doing. Ultimately, this is where you are the expert as a teacher. You know how to connect with students and parents or guardians in a way that is approachable but also professional. Here are a few ideas that I've found helpful:

1. **Social-emotional pulse check:** You can do this as a warm-up activity in your class meeting. You might begin with an open-ended question like, "How are you handling hybrid learning?" Students might meet with small breakout rooms or share their answers in the chat. Other times, you might create a more structured pulse check with something like, "Tell me two wins for the week and one disappointment." It can even be creative, where you have students create a superhero name or a band name. Some teachers have done emoji check-ins where students share an emoji to represent how they are doing. Still others have had students sketch what's on their mind or what's on their heart by drawing inside of a mind shape or a heart shape. This really depends on the age, the class culture, and the subject you teach.

2. **Video updates:** This starts with a teacher-created video. In the first week, you can do an on boarding video of the course and explain how it will work. But after that, you can create a weekly short video with a preview of what students will do. Although prerecorded, these short, unstructured videos create a sense of presence for you as a teacher. You can then ask a specific check-in question and have students send an email or fill out a survey.

3. **Video check-ins:** While it helps to create videos for students, we can also encourage students to create their own video reflections that they post for classmates. You might give students a specific prompt or provide options of multiple prompts and encourage each student to select their own prompt. Video check-ins allow students to share how their doing with body language and voice. However, the fact that they can re-record a video allows them to have a sense of control over the process.

4. **Small group check-ins:** You can schedule small group meeting and use video conferencing to meet with groups and look at their progress. Other times, you might create small groups that function as a peer advisory check-in.

5. **Email check-ups:** You can send out a whole class email with expectations, deadlines, etc. You might also send a short email to each student asking how they're doing. If you have 180 students in a class, rotate with 18 per day and make sure each student gets an individual email every other week. While this can feel overwhelming, you can create a template and personalize it.

6. **Short text check-ins:** With this option, you can ask students to use the chat function to send questions or comments as they work on various projects. Some classes might even use an option like multimedia text apps so that the check-ins remain largely asynchronous.[33]

7. **Surveys:** Ask students to fill out a course survey each week where they share what their experiences have been in a distance learning or hybrid course. These surveys tend to center on student course experience but you can also include a few questions that deal with social-emotional learning. It's important to avoid survey fatigue, so you might want to limit the surveys to 3-5 questions.

8. **Scheduled conferences:** You can schedule one-on-one video conferences with students where you guide reflection and do quick social-emotional learning check-ins. I love doing short five-minute conferences and allowing students to select between feedback conferences (where I provide help), reflection conferences (where I ask reflective questions), or assessment conferences (where I give feedback on mastery).[34]

9. **Phone calls:** This is my least favorite option because I'm an introvert and generally dislike talking on the phone. However, given the challenges students sometimes experience with internet connectivity, sometimes the best option is a simple phone call to see how a student is doing.

At this point, these options might feel overwhelming. This is why it helps to experiment with the process until you find your groove. It also helps to ask your students about their preferences for check-ins.

POLL STUDENTS FOR THE IDEAL CHECK-IN PROCESS

As an educator, you can honor student agency by asking them their preferences for check-ins. Students can submit their answers in an online form or in a short interview that you do a the beginning of the year. After students have submitted it, you can look at the spreadsheet and divide up your primary way of communicating with each student. This process sends the message that you value each student's input in their preferred approach to communication. As a result, they have a greater sense of control over frequency and method of communication. This can also free up your time to be more efficient with your communication. Not every student wants daily or weekly personalized check-ins. Some students prefer a short 3-question survey in a weekly email. Other students might need a phone call every other week.

- How can I help you? What are some areas where you might need support? What are some challenges you might have in remote learning?
- When is the best time to reach you?
- How often do you want me to communicate with you?
- What is your preferred method of communication? Do you prefer email? Chat? Phone call? Video conference?
- What type of feedback do you prefer on your work? Video feedback? Audio feedback? Comments that are typed?
- What is something former teachers have done that helped you feel known and appreciated?
- What is something former teachers have done that helped you stay on track in your course?

Students can submit their answers in an online form or in a short interview that you do at the beginning of the year. After students have submitted it, you can look at the spreadsheet and divide up your primary way of communicating with each student. This process sends the message that you value each student's input in their preferred approach to communication. As a result, they have a greater sense of control over frequency and method of communication. This can also free up your time to be more efficient with your communication. Not every student wants daily or weekly personalized check-ins. Some students prefer a short three-question survey in a weekly email. Other students might need a phone call every other week.

However, this is also a two-way process, and you might need to help students clarify expectations. You might send an email to a student affirming their desire for frequent communication but also explaining that daily one-on-one communication might be unrealistic.

Although it's important to take the initiative as the educator, it can also help to encourage students to take the initiative as well. Ultimately, empowered students should be self-advocates. Here, you might provide the ideal process for asking questions, giving feedback, and reaching out. When crafting a course syllabus, you can create a category for communicating with the teacher or professor. This category can include reasonable methods (an email, online form, office phone number), times, and expectations for when you will get back to them.

For example, as a professor, you might write the following:

Please feel free to reach out if you have questions. I am glad to help. Office hours are by appointment only. Please schedule video-conference office-hour meetings using the online Google Form in our LMS. Please feel free to email me at any time. I will be sending email updates to check in on you, and I want you to feel free to let me know if you have any questions. You can also use the chat feature in our LMS. You can generally expect a response to an email, chat, or message within twenty-four hours. I generally end my day at 5:00 p.m., so I will likely respond to a late-night email the next morning or afternoon.

However, if you are a fifth-grade teacher, it might look like this:

Please feel free to reach out if you have questions. I am glad to help. Please schedule video-conference office-hour meetings using the scheduling link in our LMS. If your parents or guardians would like to schedule a meeting, they can use the same form, or they can send me an email. Please feel free to email me at any time with questions or concerns. Also, your parent or guardian can message me directly through the recommended text app. You can generally expect a response to an email or message within twenty-four hours. If you have questions on an assignment and it's due the next day, please remember that you can always resubmit assignments after I have given feedback. Also, we will have virtual study hall sessions available to the entire class. I will be sending you a weekly check-in, and it will be really important that you read and respond each time.

Notice how both paragraphs communicate availability but also boundaries. They make it clear that you are present but they also ask students to initiate conversations.

As teachers, we can extend student empowerment beyond the learning tasks and into the community itself. This begins by building relationships and affirming students through a culturally responsive approach. It includes the use of humor and joy alongside specific structural components of design. As educators, we can work alongside students to co-create the classroom norms and procedures and to clarify the class values. As the course progresses, we can also work intentionally to engage in frequent check-ins so that students feel known.

CHAPTER 7

BOOSTING STUDENT OWNERSHIP IN
VIRTUAL
MEETINGS

Two weeks into the emergency quarantine teaching schedule, a former colleague of mine sent me a private message.

"Was I wrong to think that I knew how to build a classroom community? Have I lost the ability to be relevant? Am I no longer able to connect with kids?"

It was painful to see her reaction because I can guarantee her students love her. She's one of the best teachers I know. When I taught eighth grade, I would regularly visit her class during my prep period to observe her lessons and borrow her engagement strategies. Her classes were dynamic and interactive.

And yet . . . nobody showed up to her optional virtual meeting.

As a professor, it is common to have nobody show up to an optional meeting. My students are paying money to earn a degree. They are highly motivated. We're in a cohort model in which I teach multiple classes, and I've built relationships with them. Even then, the default is to avoid showing up to optional meetings.

At times, it can feel personal. However, that's rarely the case. Failure to show up doesn't mean students don't care. Many students don't want to feel like an imposition. Many feel they are doing okay and don't need "help" during optional office hours. Many of them are living busy lives or they're simply distracted. So, one challenge we face is students choosing not to show up to virtual meetings. But there's another challenge as well.

Virtual meetings can suffer from low engagement. Even when students show up, video chats can feel lonely. It can feel like you're talking underwater, where there's this delay in communication and a sense of separation between each person. When the microphones are all on mute, you can't hear any laughter. It's hard to read body language. Many of us would prefer to teach face to face.

However, I've grown to love virtual meetings. Even when they don't run perfectly, there are specific strategies that we can use to boost engagement and promote student ownership as we meet as a group in a synchronous video chat.

WHAT DOESN'T WORK WELL

Virtual meetings don't work well for direct instruction. If you are planning to introduce a new concept for students, your best bet would be to create an asynchronous video that they can watch and re-watch again. Instead, have students watch a prerecorded video on their own and then clarify misconceptions and take a deeper dive into the topic in a virtual meeting.

In terms of discussions, virtual meetings don't work for large class discussions. While it is feasible to have twenty students engaged in a free-flowing, face-to-face Socratic Seminar, the lack of physical space and body language makes these discussions a challenge in a virtual meeting. If you're opting for a discussion, use the breakout room functions and limit the size of the small groups to three to six students.

Virtual meetings don't tend to work well for class presentations. Often, there are logistical challenges with having students share screens, and there are quality issues if a student wants to use an embedded video clip. Instead, have students craft videos that combine annotated or recorded slideshows, live talking-head videos, clips, and visuals. Students can then watch their classmates' slideshows asynchronously and provide feedback on their own. This also allows students to edit and refine their presentation, leading to shorter, higher-quality videos. Students then have an increased amount of time to provide thoughtful feedback in the comment sections below the videos.

A general question to ask yourself is, "Could this video chat be a recorded video instead?" If the answer is "yes," then a prerecorded video is a better option. Virtual meetings tend to be dynamic and interactive while recorded videos are inherently static. So, how do we make our virtual meetings more interactive? Here are a few ideas:

- **Social or emotional check-in:** Begin your class meeting with a quick social-emotional check-in to see how students are doing. When the quarantine began, I used the prompt "quarantine band name." Students then shared their band names in the chat feature. Another time, I asked them to sketch a "high" and "low" for the week and with a quick description. Students then shared their pictures in small groups.
- **Incorporate movement:** I know of a third-grade teacher that does a daily dance to start their virtual conferences. This not only gets the blood flowing, but it also creates a shared experience. Other teachers have a class phrase or mantra or a long-distance high five that they do. These increase participation and build community.
- **Make use of hand-gestures:** Find specific hand gestures to get students moving. You might do a "four corners" activity on the screen rather than the room. Here, students place their hand by the corner they agree with, and you can provide a slide to mirror the screen. You might also use a total physical response (TPR) for content vocabulary.[35] This can help students solidify the knowledge by building an association between a word, a definition, and a movement.
- **Say their names:** This is simple but easy to forget. When calling on students, be sure to use their names. Just this simple act of hearing one's name can make a student feel known.
- **Use the Q&A feature:** Many video conference platforms have both a chat feature and a Q&A feature. The Q&A feature is a great way to create a "parking lot" where students can ask a question at any time and you, as the instructor, can check it out when the time is right.
- **Use polls:** Some video-conference platforms include a built-in poll. If that doesn't work, you can use an online poll and send the link to the students. Polls provide instant feedback and can help with reviewing information, gathering opinions, or

doing a low-stakes icebreaker. For what it's worth, I'm an introvert, so I don't enjoy breaking the ice. I'd rather it melt slowly over days or weeks.

- **Allow students to show off their pets:** If they don't have a pet, they can share a stuffed animal (preferably a "stuffy" and not a taxidermy animal) or a house plant. I did this with a recent class and a college student held out a cactus that he had named Spike. For what it's worth, my Great Dane puppy, Athena, loves to join the class in video virtual meetings whether she is invited or not. In fact, she tends to wake up and want to play precisely when class begins.
- **Use the chat function:** It can be hard to navigate a large in-person discussion. However, the chat function can allow students to share their thoughts in real-time. They can also send private chats to other classmates for a pair-share or a quick discussion.
- **Include silence:** Video conferences can still have moments for think time or for quick-writes or sketches. Simply add a timer and mute all participants to create the silence necessary for students to process the information. This benefits introverts who need personal think time to make sense out of ideas. It can also help ELL students process the language at their own pace.
- **Integrate other platforms into your virtual sessions**: It might be a shared document or an online sticky note site. A virtual meeting does not have to be locked into the specific video-conference platform. You can have students attend via video conference but then edit a shared document or co-create an infographic.
- **Use breakout rooms:** Many video conferences offer breakout rooms for small group discussions. As the instructor, you can set these groups up ahead of time or put them together in the moment.

ATHENA'S LAW

A PUPPY AT REST
WILL NO LONGER STAY AT REST
ONCE A VIDEO CALL BEGINS

DISTANCE LEARNING TRAFFIC REPORT

There's some significant slowing on Hallway 101.
Looks like two Canine Units are
investigating some misplaced cereal.
Thankfully, no accidents
to report (especially with a puppy)
but be on the look out for unexpected debris
as you reach Family Room Boulevard.
Looks like an absolute standstill
on Kitchen Avenue
due to bottlenecking by the Refrigerator.
Maybe find an alternative route
to your coffee shop.

BOOSTING ATTENDANCE IN VIRTUAL MEETINGS

Video conferences can be exhausting. You might notice that students who are highly engaged during an in-person session suddenly disengage in a virtual meeting. However, virtual class meetings can actually be a blast. I recently attended a highly interactive, dynamic fourth-grade class meeting. Students engaged in a Q&A, met in small groups, and interviewed me as an author. They had read a free book I created about a pizza with superpowers. Toward the end, each student participated in an interactive game. Students were highly engaged in the virtual meeting because the teacher had designed the entire experience using interactive elements.

The following are some strategies you can use to boost attendance in virtual meetings.

1. INVITE SPECIFIC STUDENTS WITH A PERSONAL EMAIL.

Say something like, "I could really use your participation tomorrow." Or you might provide specific feedback on an assignment and say, "It's not required but I would love for you to show up to our meeting tomorrow. I'll be reteaching it." Students want to feel wanted. You might send the email to a small group of students who need additional support. This can be framed as optional but highly recommended. While this process can take additional time, an individual email allows a student to feel known on a personal level. It feels different to receive an individualized invitation rather than an email aimed at the entire class.

2. RE-FRAME THE MEETING FROM "HELP" TO "PEER FEEDBACK."

This reduces the stigma of needing help. I had open office hours to help students with a big portfolio project, and nobody showed up. I did this for two weeks in a row and wondered if my students were just really, really advanced. Then, I changed it to an optional peer-feedback workshop and about two-thirds of the class showed up. I broke them into small groups on Zoom and then checked in with each of them. We also had a Q&A, where they began to ask for help. However, they needed to know they weren't alone in needing help. By giving peer feedback, there was a strong message that all students were still in progress. Nobody had nailed it yet. Similarly, when I meet with small groups, I rephrase it from "help" or "tutoring" to "offering feedback," and I've seen the same results.

3. ASK STUDENTS TO SHOW UP TO GIVE ME FEEDBACK ON HOW I'M DOING AS A TEACHER.

Students want to have a voice in how things are going, and it's the kind of feedback I need to improve my instruction. In user experience (UX) design, there is a core idea of asking for user feedback. Previously, I mentioned the student leadership team meetings. These are completely optional, but they provide a sense of ownership for students and an opportunity to provide meaningful feedback for the teacher.

As a teacher, I can ask about what's working and what's not working. I can also ask students for specific ideas. Afterward, we can transition into a question like, "What is still unclear for you?" or "What did I not explain well enough?" These questions lead to a place where I can re-teach core concepts or skills. At this point, the meeting begins to feel more like a true open office time.

4. PLAY A GAME TOGETHER.

I'm totally serious here. Sometimes, you need to play together for half an hour and then move into something more academic. I had a distance learning course with members of multiple cohorts. Several students knew each other well, and it created unintentional cliques. While we met on video conferencing for our official class, the small groups were distant and the conversation was stilted. At that point, I did optional hours for the next night and made it a nineties trivia night. I asked them to dress up in a nineties outfit.

That last part tanked. I get it. It was a big ask to bust out the Hammer pants. But the small-group trivia competition was the type of team-builder we needed. The next time we met for an actual virtual class session, students felt more at ease and the conversation moved smoothly.

5. DO SOMETHING HANDS-ON.

The biggest benefit from a video conference is that it's synchronous. You could do a scavenger hunt, a show-and-tell activity, or a divergent thinking activity. You could do a brain break activity in which students move around and dance. The goal is to take things off screen and allow for students to bring their world into your virtual meeting.

That being said . . . some groups have better luck with an asynchronous option. And that's okay. The biggest takeaway is that a lack of attendance has nothing to do with your value as a teacher or your relationship with students.

Teaching is deeply relational, and the physical distance makes this distance learning thing really hard at a time like this. But I think it helps to recognize that even for those of us who have been doing distance learning for years, it always takes extra effort to build and maintain community. And when the results aren't there in the way you expect them, it's not a reflection on who you are as a teacher. It's a reflection on the sheer challenge presented by distance learning itself.

SETTING THE TONE FOR VIRTUAL MEETINGS

As educators, we can take a proactive approach by setting a positive tone for virtual meetings. The following are some ways to build student ownership into the process.

NEGOTIATING NORMS

Before starting your first virtual meeting, you might want to negotiate norms as a class. If you have a larger class, you could create smaller groups that work together to create specific norms that they can then share with the larger group. Afterward, the class can negotiate the norms together. Another option is to start with an initial set of norms and allow students to annotate the norms on a shared document. They might wordsmith the norms, insert comments, and even add a few norms of their own. If you are in a hybrid environment, you could negotiate norms in person, where it is easier to engage in open dialogue. Regardless of your approach, a set of shared norms can help clarify expectations.

- **Active participation:** What does active participation look like? Have students visualize this by stating specific positive behaviors. Are students required to answer questions in the chat, or do they answer questions when they feel like it? This is why it helps to negotiate norms together as a group. It also helps to have students identify what barriers might get in the way of active participation. For example, it might be tempting to have the television on or to multitask with various tabs open.

- **Communication:** What does positive and intentional communication look like during a virtual meeting? What does it mean to use active listening skills? Note that you might ask students to mute their volume, use body language, and take turns in a virtual meeting.
- **Being prepared:** What does it mean to show up to a video chat fully prepared? For example, students might need to complete course readings, flipped videos, or a project students are working on. You might ask students to create a set of norms around starting and ending on time. You might also include a norm around testing audio and video ahead of time.
- **Staying on-topic:** You might also have some norms related to how students use the chat function, hand gestures, or other features.

A word of caution here: the goal for empowered learning is self-direction. If the norms become too restrictive, students will go through the virtual meetings with a sense of compliance. This is also why there should be a strong rationale for the norms you develop.

DEVELOPING PROCEDURES

Students can take ownership in the classroom community by helping develop the classroom procedures for video conferences. The following questions can guide the process.

- What will you use to get people's attention? In a physical classroom, you might raise your hand. But is there an option you might use in a virtual classroom meeting?

- What type of movement will you use? You might create hand gestures for certain non-verbal communication or you might have brain breaks with active movement.
- What protocols will you use for peer communication? You might incorporate private chats or breakout rooms to facilitate a think-pair-share activity.
- What will your process be for students who have unstable internet connection? You might record video chats and allow students to access them at a later date.
- Will you allow for virtual backgrounds? Some teachers find these distracting while others see virtual backgrounds as a way to promote equity because students who might be worried about a smaller apartment or a crowded space can suddenly be in a far-off galaxy or a fictional wizarding school.

Students sometimes struggle with the logistical aspects of virtual meetings. For this reason, you might spend some time going over best practices on the technical or space aspects of a virtual meeting. You can do a practice meeting where students test their video cameras and audio. It's also a chance to check for internet speed. You can help students think intentionally about lighting as well. Ideally, lighting should be in front and behind a webcam, preferably not in front of a window or under an overhead light. You can help students think about the positioning of their computers. Here you help students identify a location that works well for virtual meetings in terms of noise and distractions.

Video conferences are inherently messy. Technology won't work perfectly. Students will forget to mute themselves. Videos will freeze up. However, in-person classes are also messy. We have fire drills and announcements that interrupt us during our face-to-face lessons as well. In some ways, the challenges of a virtual meeting can help create a tighter classroom culture. These become the moments when students learn patience and show one another grace.

Virtual meetings are a great way to build community and process information in an interactive way. We can boost engagement in these virtual meetings by encouraging students to actively participate. Along the way, we can find small ways to build student ownership into the process so they experience a sense of belonging.

CHAPTER 8

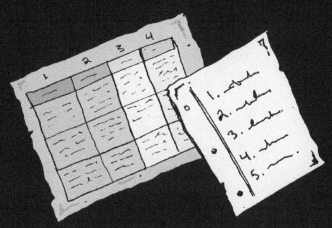

EMPOWERING STUDENTS WITH

CHOICE
AND FLEXIBILITY

While there is no instruction manual for distance learning, there are some universal ideas that can guide us as we design distance-learning experiences. One of these core ideas is student voice and choice. One of the best things we can offer students in remote learning is a sense of autonomy and control over the learning process.

However, too much choice can be a problem. Students can feel overwhelmed when things are too loose. Children need expectations, which is why agency and compliance still have a place.

As Barry Schwartz wrote in the classic *Paradox of Choice*, "Learning to choose is hard. Learning to choose well is harder.[36] And learning to choose well in a world of unlimited possibilities is harder still, perhaps too hard." We do a disservice when we provide "unlimited possibilities," because it is simply too much choice for our brains. For this reason, it can help to create structures for student choice. One option is through the design of a choice menu.

FOUR APPROACHES TO CHOICE MENUS

Choice menus have been around for years with different names, including "choice boards" and "learning menus." Regardless of the terminology, the idea is the same. Create structures that provide choices for students in their learning tasks. However, choice often exists on a spectrum from teacher-directed (less autonomy) to student-directed (more autonomy). The following graphic is a continuum of choice menus with four different levels.

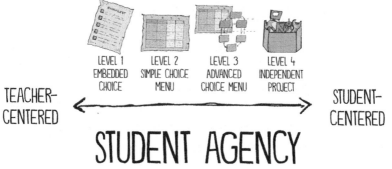

LEVEL 1
EMBEDDED
CHOICE

LEVEL 2
SIMPLE CHOICE
MENU

LEVEL 3
ADVANCED
CHOICE MENU

LEVEL 4
INDEPENDENT
PROJECT

TEACHER-
CENTERED

STUDENT-
CENTERED

STUDENT AGENCY

Note these do not have to be a progression you follow in a sequential order. You don't have to start at level 1 and then move to level 4. But, there is this idea that you may want to start at a more teacher-centered approach to get students used to the idea of choice and then move toward a level 3 or 4 over time.

LEVEL 1
EMBEDDED CHOICE

Choice Level:
Mostly Teacher-Directed

Description:
With this first level, students all work on the same main assignment or project. Here, every student is working on the same learning targets and tasks for the majority of the assignment. The entire class has common grouping (individual, partners, or small groups) and generally works at the same pace. However, within this assignment, the teacher provides options on a sub-task.

So, in a language arts class, the entire class might do the same reading and answer similar questions. However, the teacher might include a menu of options for how students present their answers. They might record a podcast, make a slideshow, do a sketchnote, film a video, or write a blog post. Another variation of this might be that every student is writing a blog post, but they have a list of topics they can select. So, they don't have a choice in the final product, but they do have a choice in the topic.

In a math class, students might have the same set of word problems, but they select from a menu of options. Here, they might select three different word problems or two algorithms. Or, they might work on the same word problem but have a menu of strategies they select for how they solve the problems. For linear equations, this might include graphing, creating a table, or using an algorithm. Another time, they might all solve the same problem, but they have a choice in how they share their answers with classmates.

The core idea is that most of the assignment is the same but there is one element with an embedded choice menu. This is ideal when you first introduce a concept or skill and you want to make sure every student has the background knowledge they need before moving on.

LEVEL 2
SIMPLE CHOICE MENU

Choice Level:
Somewhat Student-Directed

Description:
This builds on the last idea with a key variation. Instead of having a common assignment and embedded choices, students have a common learning target but a set of options for which assignments they choose. This might include choices in grouping, choices in topics, and choices in the products they create. So, students might do independent reading with whatever novels they choose to read. Afterward, they can select any number of book report prompts that the teacher provides.

BOOK REVIEW CHOICE MENU

BOOK REVIEW   BOOK TRAILER   BOOK REVIEW   BOOK CLUB
PODCAST   VIDEO   BLOG POST   WITH STUDY GUIDE

The simple choice menu is ideal for a classroom where students are all mastering the same standard. If the standard is skill-based but topic-neutral, students have leeway in choosing their own topics (or choosing from a list of topics) but less freedom in the skills they practice. Other times, the standard might be topic-based and conceptual but there is more freedom in the skills students master and the products they create. Here, students might learn about World War II, but the simple choice menu could include making a comic book, creating a virtual museum, or doing a diary of a soldier.

Another variation of this is the tic-tac-toe option. Here, students select an assignment in each row to get a "tic-tac-toe" for a completed assignment. The key idea is that there is a common learning target but freedom in everything else.[37]

LEVEL 3
ADVANCED CHOICE MENU

Choice Level:
Mostly Student-Directed

Description:
Advanced choice menus take the last idea another step further by having students self-select the standards or learning targets along with their final product where they demonstrate their learning. The following is an example of an advanced choice menu. Students begin by selecting their grouping (partners, small group, or independent). Next, they select the specific learning targets. This is ideal for students who need additional review of certain content. It functions as a built-in intervention. After deciding on the

learning target, students find related resources that they explore connected to the learning target. These might be tutorials, examples, articles, podcasts, or videos. Finally, students select from options in how they will present their learning.

In a math class, you might have a student choose to work with a partner. Both partners decide to work on dividing fractions. When they look at the list of curated resources, one partner chooses to watch a tutorial video while another partner chooses to read an online tutorial. Next, they complete a task in which they divide fractions and then they select the video option where they show how they solved the problems together. Although they are working miles away from each other, they are able to share their videos with one another and with their teacher,

While the table works well for this option, a more advanced variation would be to do it as an online form, with students selecting an option that leads to a new set of options.

Note that this option works best with secondary students who have a solid background knowledge of their topics or a solid understanding of the skills. This type of choice menu can easily overwhelm students, which is why you might start out with one of the first two options before moving to this one.

LEVEL 4
INDEPENDENT PROJECT

Choice Level:
Entirely Student-Directed

Description:
Independent projects require a shift from choice to freedom. Instead of relying on teachers to provide a menu of options,

students select the grouping, decide on the topics, ask their own questions, engage in their own research, find their own resources (rather than selecting from a curation), and ultimately create their own products.

One option is a Genius Hour project. Based on the Google concept of 20% time, the goal is to provide students with 20% of their class time to learn what they want. They choose the content while also mastering skills and hitting the academic standards.[38]

With Genius Hour, students own the entire journey. They choose the topics based on their own geeky interests. It doesn't have to be a traditionally academic area. They might like fashion or food or sports or Legos or Minecraft or deep-sea creatures. They can then match these topics with topic-neutral standards. Students ask the questions and engage in their own research to find the answers. Along the way, they design their own plan of instruction. They decide which resources to use and which activities to pursue. Each student sets goals and engages in self-assessment. They work at their own pace and set their own deadlines. Students decide on the grouping. Some work alone. Others work in pairs or small groups. In the end, students figure out what they will make and how they will share their learning with the world.

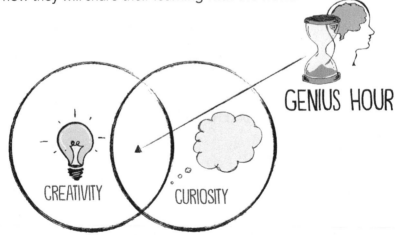

GENIUS HOUR

CREATIVITY

CURIOSITY

A word of caution: It's not a free for all. The best Genius Hour projects have systems and structures that empower students to reach their full potential. I find it helpful to break genius hour into phases and have students document it with a Genius Hour journal. This could be done on an online document or it could be done as a podcast or video.

Another option would be something like a Wonder Day[39] project, where students can choose their grouping, choose their topics, create their own questions, engage in research, and ultimately create either a podcast, video, slideshow, or blog post where they share their findings. This concept also fits within the key area of having students own their curiosity, which we will explore in a future chapter. Here's a chart you can use to help walk students through the choices.

Wonder Day Choices

Phase	Choice
Grouping	Will you work individually, in pairs, or in small groups?
Question	What is your question? Write it here.
Research	What are your sources? List them below.
Product	What is your product? Your options include podcast, blog post, presentation, or video.

GETTING STARTED WITH CHOICE MENUS

Choice boards are most often used in the early elementary levels. Do a simple online search of choice menus, and you'll see plenty of examples for second- and third-grade classrooms. However, student choice should increase as students grow more mature and responsible. Young adults have a natural drive for independence and choice menus can be a way to affirm their autonomy and provide choice.

One of the biggest challenges at the high school and collegiate level is the sheer amount of content students must learn. However, it helps to examine the standards and ask where student choice is most evident. It might be in the option of an assignment or in the way a student presents their learning. Other times, there might be more flexibility in selecting topics or in choosing strategies and methods. A math choice menu might involve selecting certain problems to solve or choosing from a bank of strategies. You might ask students to craft their own problems (an idea we explore in a future chapter). By contrast, a history choice menu might involve choosing what kind of content to create (a video, podcast, or blog), what subtopic to explore, or what question to ask. This simple exercise can open up new opportunities in crafting choice menus. You might even reach out to students and ask for ideas of tasks or assignments they would want in a choice menu.

Ultimately, student choice is a long journey, and it varies from student to student. Some students might be at a place where they can only handle the first or second levels of choice menus — and that's okay. The important thing is that they are seeing how much you are honoring their autonomy as learners. In the end, when we provide students with choice, they are empowered to become self-directed learners, engaging in creativity and critical thinking.

CHAPTER 9

EMPOWERING STUDENTS
TO PURSUE THEIR
INTERESTS

As an educator, you work hard to make courses interesting. You find specific strategies that get students excited and engaged. You find stories that will pique their interests and use examples that feel relevant to students' lives. If you're a professor, you fight hard against the stereotype of the dry lecture. You craft interactive lectures and speak with passion and energy. If you're a middle-school math teacher, you fight against the stereotypes of math as a "boring" subject, and you actively work toward reducing math anxiety. For your students, math is a playground. As a high-school English teacher, you make Shakespeare relevant for the moment, and as a fifth-grade social studies teacher, you demonstrate how events from the past are still impacting the present day.

We want our students to fall in love with the subjects we teach. Regardless of the grade level or the context, we are constantly finding ways to make our lessons more interesting. In an online setting, it might involve finding fascinating articles or podcasts. You might find new stories or examples that you incorporate into your videos.

While it's important to make courses interesting, it is also important to craft moments when students can pursue their interests and passions. Instead of simply making a lesson interesting, we are asking students, "What do you find interesting?" and then connecting this to the subjects we teach. In these moments, students feel empowered to own their learning because they have a sense of agency over the topics they are exploring.

The following are some reasons to tap into student interests:

1. Starting with student interests can help build student confidence. Certain students might struggle with a particular skill or concept. They might arrive to your class feeling like they are behind. However, when they pursue their interests, they build on their own expertise and gain greater confidence in your classroom.

2. Starting with student interests affirms their agency. As the instructor, you are saying, "I want you to share your expertise. I don't care if people think it's shallow or insignificant. Who you are matters to me. So, if you geek out about Hello Kitty or limericks or super spicy pepper jams, I want you to share it."

3. Starting with student interests sends the message that we are all experts in something. This creates a culture where students are able to learn from one another from day one. It's also a chance to be humble and model the learning process for your students.

4. Starting with student interests can be a safe way to get to know one another. Not every student feels safe sharing their story. Starting with a personal biography or a comprehensive get-to-know-you activity can create situations where students re-live trauma.[40] While vulnerability has a place in the classroom, it can take months to develop trust as a community, and students should have a sense of control over how much they are sharing. Furthermore, some students don't feel safe sharing aspects of their identity. This is especially true for certain members of the LGBT+ community. However, everyone has geeky interests and sharing geeky interests allows students to share something personal without centering it on their story or their identity.

5. By starting with student interests, you are able to create a bridge between the subject area you teach and each student's world. As a result, they are able to see the subject area matter as inherently relevant to their lives.

The following are a few strategies you can use in a hybrid or remote learning environment to tap into student interests.

A SHOW-AND-TELL APPROACH

When the quarantine first began, I wanted to create a situation where students could share their geeky interests while also processing healthy ways of dealing with social isolation. I began our class video conference with the following prompt:

CHOOSE ONE ITEM

Choose one item that represents a healthy way that you are dealing with social isolation. It could be a hobby, a mindset, or a creative endeavor. Explain why you chose that item.

I then gave students ninety seconds to find an item of their choosing. When that was done, I called on each student using a randomizer and asked students to explain their object. Each student had two minutes to talk about their item, which meant we were potentially going to spend nearly an hour on this activity. It felt like a gamble.

I was nervous about this. After all, these were graduate students in their final course. However, it was awesome. One student grabbed a guitar and played a few riffs for us. Another student grabbed a giant mixer (she probably could have moved her laptop instead) and then explained what it was like to rekindle her love of baking by doing recipes alongside her grandmother using FaceTime. Still, another described getting into painting for the first time ever. One by one, each student gave us a small look into their world. It was powerful.

This was a healthy opportunity for students to open up about their experiences and their emotions. Some chose to stick to the function of their item but others used it as a way to share a core part of their identity. Each time a student shared an item, it felt like a gift to the entire community. This is now my go-to opening-day activity in virtual courses.

A variation on this activity is to have students select their item and create a one-minute prerecorded video that they post to the class LMS. Students can then comment on their classmates' videos.

GEEK OUT BLOGS

I previously mentioned Genius Hour as a way to tap into taking student choice to the next level. However, there is another variation of this process, in the form of the Geek Out Blog.[41] I start with the following questions:

1. What do you really care about? Why?
2. What is something that you're passionate about?
3. What is something you know inside and out?
4. What are some things you believe deeply in? What are some convictions you have about life?
5. What do you love to do?
6. What do you know a lot about?
7. If you could invent your own course, what would it be?

I explain that geekiness is a passion, interest, enjoyment, and often conviction about a particular topic. I then give them stems they could use:

- Seven Reasons Why _____
- Seven Ways to _____
- Seven Things to Know about _____
- Seven Best _____
- The Seven (Adjective) _____ in _____

Over the years, student answers have been all over the place. A girl chose Korean pop music while the girl next to her delved into issues of immigration. In the same class, another student chose Minecraft while the kid next to him gave seven amazing reasons why zombies would make great pets. A few kids wrote about their lives, their families, or their cultures.

It's also a way to model digital citizenship and digital ethics in a way that builds community and affirms each student's identity.

SCAVENGER HUNT

A scavenger hunt is similar to the show-and-tell concept. Here, teachers give students specific clues or items that they find from their homes. This works well as a video-conference activity, but it can also work as a series of photos that students take and upload to a shared file. Students can work in teams using the breakout room function, or they can work independently. The following are a few scavenger hunt ideas:

- **Math scavenger hunt:** Students find specific items in their homes that connect to core math concepts. They might even measure certain items and report back to the group.
- **Maker scavenger hunt:** Teachers give students a list of item specifications. It might be something soft, something elastic, something round, etc. After they have found those items, they get a set amount of time to create something new with those items.
- **Science hunt:** When students are learning about natural environments, they might use their phones to take snapshots of different environments in their neighborhood. I've seen teachers go as advanced as birding, with key coordinates and pictures or using this process with astronomy or meteorology. But it can also be something simpler, like finding predators and prey.
- **History hunt:** Students can do a walk of their city and find elements of culture or find identifiers of history (such as street names or plaques).
- **Language Arts scavenger hunt:** At a younger age, students might explore environmental texts. They can search for sight words on something like a cereal box. They might take a picture of that word and upload it to the class LMS or a teacher might give them the challenge to "find a word that ends with a silent-e." With older grades, students might find themes or genres on the larger community.
- **P.E. scavenger hunt:** Students might have a set of challenges where they have to hop to certain items and then do a series of jumping jacks when they find another item. Students can record their movements on a phone as evidence of their exercise.
- **Music scavenger hunt:** Students can do a scavenger hunt where they have to record certain types of music that they hear in the environment. Or a simpler version might involve

finding something that can create a percussion, a string sound, etc.

UNCONFERENCE

Popularized by EdCamps,[42] unconferences are open-ended, interest-driven conferences that typically happen in person. However, they can also work well in a remote-learning format. The unconference process begins with participants brainstorming a list of topics or ideas. Often, the group will then vote for topics they prefer. A quick way to vote might be with a shared form tied to email addresses (to avoid duplicate votes), but a quick online poll can also work. Finally, they engage in a free-flowing open conversation. In some cases, you might have a discussion leader who facilitates.

In a remote environment, a teacher or professor might choose any of the following formats:

- **Twitter chat**: This is typically fast paced and highly interactive. Often, you'll have a larger group of participants. However, it is also public, which means there are issues of privacy. In the U.S., for example, a Twitter chat mentioning the name of a course might be a Family Educational Rights and Privacy Act (FERPA) violation.[43] A Twitter chat can have specific questions set up ahead of time, or it can be a free-flowing conversation.
- **Discussion board**: This is a little more old-school, but using the discussion board or forum option on an LMS can allow you to set up your unconference topics as specific forum topics. Students can then respond to one another in a way that is threaded (a person writes and their responses are nested underneath the initial response) or unthreaded (it reads like a

linear chat conversation). A discussion board should be limited to no more than ten people before it becomes hard to track.

- **Walkie-Talkie Conversation:** Students can use a walkie-talkie app to engage in an ongoing discussion.[44] This can exist at a dedicated time or over a longer period of time. The key here is that they can speak or write.

- **Video Chat:** Students can meet using the preferred video conferencing method and discuss the topic with either pre-set questions or in a style closer to a Socratic Seminar. These video chats work best with three to four participants, so that it is still easy to read body language and manage communication.

HOW-TO VIDEOS

Students often arrive to class with certain practical skills. One way for them to share their expertise is through short how-to videos or articles. This option works well in an English or communications course, where teachers can tie this into standards relating to functional and instructional texts. However, it can also work in any performance-based subject, including art, physical education, drama, filmmaking, photography, and music.

The idea is for students to create step-by-step videos where they can teach classmates a specific skill or strategy. This honors students' expertise while also allowing them to deepen their learning by teaching the skill to others. It also helps them gain empathy while improving their communication skills.

Certain students might feel as though they are not experts in anything. In these moments, it might help to give examples of small hacks that they might want to share. They might know how to tie a certain knot or have a fun way to repurpose items around the house. Many students will have small skills, hacks, or processes that don't seem like a big deal. However, as they share their how-to videos, they are often surprised by just how many people find the videos helpful.

Students can house these videos in a shared folder or within the class LMS. However, they might also want to publish their how-to videos online as well.

HOW DO YOU ALIGN STUDENT INTERESTS WITH THE CONTENT STANDARDS?

Whenever I mention interest-based activities, people ask, "How do you get away with teaching whatever topics you want?"

The simple answer is, I'm not teaching whatever topics I want. The students are choosing the topics, and they're able to do so because the standards are topic-neutral. For example, in our Geek Out Blogs, my middle-school students had to make sure that their blogs included persuasive and explanatory texts.

This project included nearly every single reading and writing standard in the first few weeks of school. Notice how none of those standards mention specific topics. Students could choose skateboarding or fashion or history or video games and still work toward mastering the same skill-based standards as their classmates.

While some standards are content-neutral, other standards require you to teach very specific concepts, topics, and ideas. What happens, for example, when you have to teach about force and acceleration or linear equations or World War II? In these moments, it helps to do a choice audit of your standards. Ask the following questions:

- **Is it possible for students to choose the topics or the content, even within the parameters of the unit plan?** For example, if the topic is adaptations and ecosystems in biology, could students choose an ecosystem that interests them? Could they focus on one specific organism? Could they find a subtopic, such as specific ways deep-sea creatures have adapted to their environment?

- **What choices could students have around the strategies they use?** So, if the topic is tighter, can they have additional choice in their approach to how they learn about it? For example, could they choose between podcasts, videos, and articles?

- **Are students able to choose their own formats (multimedia, for example)?** If the subject is bound by a tight curriculum in K-12 or a tight set of course goals in a college syllabus, can they choose what type of content they create? Note that this isn't about learning styles. There is no difference between an auditory or visual learner. We are all auditory, visual, kinesthetic, etc. This is about asking what type of content creation students are most interested in creating.

- **Is this something that students can practice throughout the year, or does it have to be confined to one particular unit?** If students are working remotely or in a hybrid environment, they might have more flexibility in schedules. This would enable them to pursue interest-based projects and activities when they have already mastered other standards. It would work as an enrichment activity.

After doing a choice audit, teachers might find ways for students to pursue their interests within a topic. So, in a science course on chemical reactions, students might be interested in chemical reactions in cooking or baking. It still fits within the standards, but students are choosing a topic and an applied context. Students might be studying World War I, but one group researches women's rights during that era while another looks at battle tactics and another group explores art, culture, and music of the era (relating how the war impacted modernism).

In some cases, topic-driven courses might also contain topic-neutral standards. This might include the scientific method in science and historical research methods (including how to read primary and secondary sources, how to create a timeline, and how to engage in historical reasoning).

Note, too, that many interest-driven assignments also have components or inquiry-based learning. When students create a science-fair project or a history-day project, they are choosing their own topic but also working through the inquiry process.

As educators, we don't always have many choices about course goals or content standards. However, we can work within these constraints to find key areas where students can pursue their interests. And when this happens, students are able to connect the subject you teach to each students' world. As a result, see the relevance of the topics you teach.

CHAPTER 10

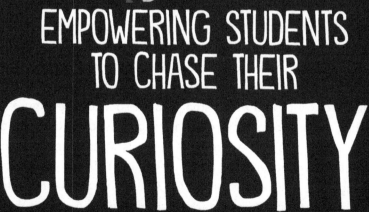

EMPOWERING STUDENTS
TO CHASE THEIR
CURIOSITY

As humans, we are naturally curious. Spend ten minutes with a toddler, and you'll face a barrage of questions. However, as they grow older, students often internalize the importance of answering questions rather than questioning answers. The school system tends to place a high premium on getting the right answer quickly and staying on-topic.

As a result, students grow less curious and more focused on proving their knowledge. They grow risk-averse about asking questions, often viewing curiosity as a sign of weakness. As teachers, we can design our virtual and hybrid courses to cultivate student curiosity. However, it isn't as simple as saying, "Hey everyone, you need to ask more questions." It requires intentional design on the part of the instructor.

As educators, we can promote student curiosity by creating a culture of inquiry. This begins by modeling the inquiry process. As an instructor, you can pose questions and walk students through the process of gathering data and drawing conclusions. As you model the process, it's also important to provide sentence frames and sample sentences for students. You can house these on a set of shared documents online that students can copy and paste. You might also include them in an online infographic or in a slideshow that students can easily access within the course tutorials.

Frequency is critical here. It helps to integrate student questions into every lesson. As you teach a new concept, you might create spaces where students can ask clarifying questions. In a virtual meeting, students could type their questions in a chat or do a quick breakout room where small groups spend three minutes generating a brainstorm of current clarifying questions. Another option is an anonymous online form, where students can submit clarifying questions whenever they need clarification. Some video-conferencing apps have a specialized Q&A function where students can submit questions, but you might also have a Q&A area in the LMS as well. The following sample questions can help students who struggle with asking clarifying questions.

- What process did you use? Why did you choose to use that process?
- How did you make that? What was your thinking behind it?
- What clues helped you find that?
- Can you explain what you were thinking?
- What part was challenging for you? How did you get past the challenge?

In addition, you might create spaces where students can pose critical-thinking questions to one another. It might be an asynchronous online forum where students pose open-ended questions and share their thoughts in an ongoing dialogue. They could also engage in these discussions via a walkie-talkie app, an asynchronous video app[45] or a chat.[46] If you're using an online forum or discussion board, it helps to choose a threaded option and requires students to ask at least one question to their classmates rather than simply leave comments.[47]

This can feel a little stilted and artificial at first. However, as students get into the habit of asking questions, they find a natural flow, and you can pull back the requirement of asking questions.

For a synchronous option, you might create small-group discussions with a focus on having students ask probing, clarifying, and critical thinking questions. These become dynamic alternatives to the Socratic Seminars, class discussions, and philosophical explorations that you can do in-person.

You can also integrate these critical questions into a lesson by asking students to post their "wonderings" within a lesson. You might take a break within a virtual meeting and have students go to an "I wonder" shared document or a virtual board where they can add sticky notes.[48] From there, you can answer questions as an instructor, or you can give students a dedicated time to research the answers and share their findings with the class. It can help to provide critical-thinking question stems, including the following:

- What evidence can you present for or against _____?
- How does _____ contrast with _____?
- What is the significance of _____?
- What distinction would you make between _____ and _____?
- Why is _____?
- What are the pros and cons of _____?
- What are the advantages of _____?

Other times, you might create sample questions they can use and practice. Students can then modify these questions to make them their own. Here are some sample questions you might provide for students:

- Why does your process work? Is there a scenario where that might not work?
- What can you do to prove to me that your process was correct?
- Is there another way to look at this?
- How did you arrive at that conclusion?
- Is there a more efficient way to do this process?

Another approach is to have students ask diagnostic questions to one another. In a language arts class, students might ask questions to solicit feedback on a piece of writing. In math, it might be a diagnostic question to determine why they missed a problem or to compare and contrast strategies. The following sentence frames can help facilitate the process:

- What did you do to get to _____?
- What part are you struggling with? Can you elaborate on _____?
- What part isn't working?
- How would you refine or improve _____?
- Is there another strategy you can use to _____?
- What do you already know about _____?
- Can you build on _____?
- What information are you missing in _____?
- Would it be more effective if you _____?

Students should ask questions to one another as they share their work. So, rather than merely leaving a comment on a blog post or a video, you can encourage students to ask questions that will then encourage students to clarify their ideas and explain their thinking to classmates. You might use questions frames such as the following:

- Why did you _____?
- What made you think of writing _____?
- Have you considered _____?
- Is it possible that _____?
- Have you considered the possibility that _____?
- I was wondering why _____?
- I was a little confused about _____.
- Could you explain _____?

Ultimately, though, if we want students to own the inquiry process, we need to create larger inquiry-based lessons and projects in which students have the opportunity to ask questions, engage in research, analyze their findings, and share their conclusions with others.

INQUIRY-BASED ACTIVITIES

Inquiry-based learning has existed for thousands of years, which makes it hard to pin down as a specific learning theory. Essentially, any time students are pursuing their questions and discovering answers, they are engaged in the inquiry process. Theorists often conceptualize the inquiry process as a cycle beginning with a provocation or core idea that sparks their curiosity.[49] This helps activate their prior knowledge. Students then ask questions, which spark their research. In this research phase, they might engage in interviews, find online sources, or conduct an experiment. This leads to a phase where students analyze data or organize their information and draw key conclusions. From here, they communicate their answers with a larger audience and reflect on their learning. This often works as a new provocation, which leads to new questions.

Sometimes students need a gradual release approach to inquiry. Heather Banchi and Randy Bell define four different types of inquiry that you can view on a spectrum from teacher-centered and structured, to learner-centered and open.[50]

- Level 1 is confirmation inquiry, where the teacher teaches the concepts, creates the questions, and models the process for students.
- Level 2 is structured inquiry, where the teacher creates the initial questions and shares the procedures, then students walk through the rest of the inquiry process by collecting data, analyzing data, and drawing conclusions.
- Level 3 is guided inquiry, where the teacher provides the research questions but students own the research or experimentation process.
- Level 4 is open/true inquiry. Here students formulate their own questions, design their own experiments or research, collect their own data, and share their findings.

According to Banchi and Bell, teachers should start with levels 1 and 2 and use those as scaffolding, so that students can learn the inquiry process. However, the inquiry process varies from subject to subject. Historical inquiry doesn't look quite the same as an experimental scientific inquiry. Age and background knowledge also play a role. Students can own more of the inquiry process when they have a deeper conceptual understanding of the content.

In a remote-learning environment, the instructor might start level 1 as a video conference modeling the process. The teacher might pause and ask students to share their own questions in the chat feature. Another option might be a prerecorded video walking students through the inquiry process and sharing the rationale for each step. This might be a specific step-by-step science lab (What happens to a balloon when heat is applied?), a topic in history (What caused the rise of imperialism?), or a mathematical concept (How do you make statistical predictions?).

For level 2, a teacher could create a set of research questions on a shared document but also ask students to add some additional questions. Students could then meet in teams to gather and analyze data. This phase could be done synchronously in a video chat or asynchronously using a shared document or spreadsheet. Afterward, the whole class could meet together to share their results and conclusions via a video conference.

For level 3, the instructor would start with a set of guided questions. Students would add their own follow-up questions or clarifying questions to the shared document online. They might even make predictions. This initial phase could occur in a video chat or on the LMS. In a synchronous video chat, the teacher might use the breakout rooms to have students clarify their process for gathering and analyzing data (i.e., doing online research, interviewing people, solving a problem, doing an experiment). Next, they could work collaboratively for the data gathering and research phases. They could then share their conclusions with the whole class synchronously in a video conference or asynchronously through a blog post, video, or podcast.

For level 4, the instructor might begin with a general provocation for inquiry. It might be a picture, a video, or a written scenario that sets the tone for the inquiry process. Teachers might keep it entirely open by asking students to pursue any question within a specific topic or subject. So, students might ask any question they want about the way gravity works in science or about the history of video games in social studies. Next, students could work individually, in pairs, or in teams to set up their process for gathering and analyzing data. Finally, they could share their question, process, data, and conclusions in the form of a multimedia composition. The following are specific examples of open inquiry projects in different subject areas.

- **What can you do with this? (math):** I love this concept from math education expert Dan Meyer.[51] As a teacher, you provide a picture or video that provokes student curiosity. Some of the best pictures or videos get students asking, "What would happen if _____?" or "Will _____ make it into _____?" You then ask students to develop their own math questions that they then solve. In doing so, they develop mathematical reasoning while also seeing how real-world inquiry works in math.

- **Testing urban legends (science):** There are so many examples of open inquiry projects in science. The most well-known would be the science-fair project. However, any student-initiated science experiment would fit into this category. One of my favorite examples is a *Mythbusters*-inspired project, where students take an urban legend or science myth and see if it's true.[52] They can design a science project that will answer the question.

- **Student journalism projects (language arts):** There are many options for inquiry in language arts because the subject is skill-based and the standards are topic-neutral. So, students can do a Wonder Day project, and it fits in nicely with the English / language arts (ELA) standards. However, another option is a student journalism project, where students ask a question about their world and engage in research, where they read articles, interview people, and ultimately cite evidence as they compose a newspaper article, blog post, podcast episode, or video.

- **PSA project (social studies):** Students can find a specific social issue and engage in the inquiry process to determine the causes and effects of the health issue. They then present what they learned in the form of a public service announcement (PSA) flier or video.

These are just a few examples. National Science Fair[53] and National History Day[54] projects are examples of larger inquiry-based projects that also connect to bigger competitions. However, certain inquiry-based projects can be interdisciplinary. One example is the Curiosity Cast, an inquiry-based podcast project.

LAUNCH A CURIOSITY CAST

Step 1: Students begin with a topic. It might be connected to a particular theme or unit of study. However, it might simply be a random topic they choose. In a history class, students might ask questions about the Mayan civilization, or they might choose a random topic in history, such as the history of skateboarding or the history of trap music. In science, they might choose a subtopic about weather, or they might simply ask any big science questions. Individually, students generate the topic on their own and add it to a shared document. When duplicate topics emerge, students then have the opportunity to work in pairs or small groups (no larger than four). Ultimately, each student chooses both the grouping and the topic for their podcast. This process is inherently messy, but it can help increase student buy-in and ownership from the start.

Step 2: Students generate a set of research questions connected to their topic. As a teacher, you can provide them with research sentence frames. You might include this on a slideshow or in a shared document that they can copy and paste.

Step 3: Students provide feedback on one another's questions. Students are looking for the following:

- This question is specific.
- This question is on-topic.
- This question will allow you to find facts rather than just opinions.

The method of feedback can vary depending on the technology and the grouping. If it's a blended classroom, students might provide feedback in person. If they're working remotely, students can choose between leaving feedback as comments asynchronously on a shared document, recorded video feedback, or in an email. They can also give feedback synchronously with a phone call, a walkie-talkie app, or a video conference.

Step 4: Students engage in online research. A key benefit of working remotely is students can read at their own pace, and they're not tied to a tight class schedule. However, this also means you might have to create some accountability, so you might ask students to find at least five facts or answer at least two of their questions. In this research phase, students can organize their information in whatever style works best for them. They might use a spreadsheet, a table, a set of notecards, or create a sketchnote. This phase will vary from student to student. Some students might need additional support, including a small-group video conference or a mini-lesson on the research process.

Step 5: Students share their information with a partner or small group. This works well as a video conference, with teachers clarifying expectations and then asking students to move into breakout rooms. However, a quicker option might be a simple email update or a comment on the class LMS. If students are working individually, this is an opportunity to share their findings with someone who has had no background knowledge. This process of sharing and clarifying information can lead to better research on the second day. Meanwhile, if students are working in teams, it's an opportunity to share their findings and expand their knowledge as a group.

Step 6: Students go in-depth in research for a second or even third day. The goal is to develop a rich understanding of the topic. You might ask students to create concept maps, which they can do by hand or using an online app.

Step 7: Students share their work in a podcast. They can use a dedicated remote podcasting app or create a video recording and then take the audio out afterward using an audio editor. If the technology process seems too complicated, you might simply make it a vodcast and have students record their video chat.

If students are in a small group, they can stick to a single topic. If students worked individually, they can share their findings with a partner. The following is a sample outline of a curiosity cast between two partners who both worked on their own separate individual research topics:

- Partner A and B both introduce their topic and explain why they chose them.
- Partner A introduces the questions and shares the research process.
- Partner B asks any clarifying questions that might guide the story.
- Partner A shares the answers as well as any fascinating facts.
- Partner A and B can have an open discussion about the findings, facts, and other questions they might have.
- Partner B introduces the questions and shares the research process.

- Partner A asks any clarifying questions that might guide the story.
- Partner B shares the answers as well as any fascinating facts.
- Partner B and A can have an open discussion about the findings, facts, and other questions they might have.

Although this is a general outline, partners should feel the flexibility to modify this. The following is a small group outline where the entire group had the same topic:

- The group shares their questions and each member talks about why they chose the topic.
- Each group shares what questions they asked and what answers they found.
- As they share their facts, other group members can add additional facts or explanations. It should feel like a conversation.
- Each member shares one fascinating fact that surprised them.
- They end with each member either sharing a new question they have or why they think their findings matter.

Again, the outline is meant to be flexible. If groups do subsequent curiosity casts, it becomes an easier process.

MAKING INQUIRY A PRIORITY

The inquiry process is a key component in nearly every discipline and domain. It's a key aspect of the scientific method. It's also how engineers and mathematicians solve key problems. Inquiry is how we make sense out of the world in journalism and in writing and it often sparks discoveries in history, anthropology, and sociology. Some of the most significant innovations began with a nagging question or a small curiosity, which is why inquiry is so important for entrepreneurial thinking.

As educators, we can empower students to own the inquiry process. It starts by being intentional about having students ask questions throughout our virtual meetings and within our online assignments. You can also take curiosity to the next level by piloting smaller inquiry-based learning expeditions or devote extended time to longer inquiry-based projects. Ultimately, when students chase their curiosity, the inquiry process becomes a lifelong habit, and students grow into innovators and problem-solvers who change the world.

CHAPTER 11

EMPOWERING STUDENTS TO OWN THE CREATIVE PROCESS

In education, we often use consumer language to describe instruction. How do you deliver the lesson? Did the students get it? There's some truth to this. We need to engage in direct instruction. We often model a particular skill that students then copy. Other times, we help students attain knowledge by reading articles, watching videos, or listening to lectures. So, on some level, we ask students to consume content that we share.

However, we also want students to be problem-solvers and makers and designers. In other words, we want students to develop a maker mindset. This is why students need to own the creative process in remote and hybrid courses. This includes the following:

- **Problem-solving:** Students need the opportunity to solve authentic problems by applying their own strategies to situations and scenarios.
- **Synthesizing:** Creative thinking isn't always hands-on. Sometimes, it's a matter of synthesizing information from multiple sources and gaining a new perspective. Students might apply an idea or process from one domain to another domain. Often, students create mashups between multiple sources.
- **Iterative thinking:** Students should have the opportunity to revise and refine a product through trial and error. This might be a specific prototype they create, but it could also involve an action, a process, or a service. When they own the iterative process, they get the opportunity to analyze what is working and failing before planning out the next iteration.
- **Ideation:** It's not uncommon to see a creative project where each student has essentially designed the exact same product. However, when they own the ideation process, they are generating their own ideas. They then narrow down the ideas and develop a specific plan for a prototype.

- **Prototyping:** Students need opportunities to create proto-types that they can test and revise. These prototypes might be digital or physical products. However, they might be a service, action, or performance. In some cases, a prototype might be a system or a process.
- **Divergent thinking:** Students need opportunities to think outside the box. With divergent thinking, they can solve problems using creative constraints by generating multiple ideas and making connections between seemingly unrelated ideas.

BUT WHAT DOES THIS ACTUALLY LOOK LIKE?

In this chapter, we explore specific ways that we can empower students to own the creative process.

BLOGGING

Thematic blogs are blogs based on a student's interests, passions, and ideas. In the case of the previously mentioned Geek Out Blogs, it could be a foodie blog, a sports blog, a fashion blog, a science blog, or a history blog. They choose the topic and the audience. It's a great way for students to practice writing in different genres (persuasive, functional, informational/expository, narrative) with specific blog topics they choose. They can also add multimedia components, such as slideshows, pictures, videos, and audio.

Blogging provides students with the opportunity to participate in the global blogging community by tapping into their own expertise and interests. If you're interested in getting started, I have included things like sentence stems and other student handouts that might be helpful as you begin the process.

Blogging is content-neutral, so you might have students create a history of fashion blog for social studies or a "math in real life" blog for math. In ELA, they might do blogging as a form of literature circles. However, it's important that public blogs respect student privacy. In the U.S., it could be a FERPA violation to create a class blog that includes student names because the end result would be the sharing of a public record.

PODCASTING

With podcasts, students create audio recordings that they then share with an authentic audience. They can work individually, with partners, or in small groups. The delivery can be more scripted or more open, depending on each student's comfort level. If you want, you can have students edit the podcasts and add music by using music editing software.[55] However, you can also do a simple recording with smartphones. Curious about what this looks like? Here are some ideas.

1. THIS IS THE FUTURE

Grades: 9-12

Students begin by asking questions about what the future will be like, such as "Will we have flying cars?" or "What will the environment be like?" or "Will robots replace all of our jobs?" or "How will cities change with self-driving cars?" They then engage in in-depth research about everything from social trends to politics to globalization to technology. In the end, they engage in a discussion in which they tackle different key questions about the future they will inhabit.

2. BOOK REVIEW

Grades: 3-12

Students can write out a script for an engaging book review and then read it into their smartphone. They can review the plot, setting, conflict, theme, and pacing. Then, they can give it a rating and discuss what type of reader they would recommend it for. It's simple but highly engaging. Another variation is to do an ongoing literature circle podcast in which students run the podcast series like an audio book club (which would work well at the secondary level).

You can also take a more creative approach and have students do creative prompts connected to the book. Students might interview a character. Here, one student takes on the role of the interviewer, and the other student takes the role of a character in the story in a Q&A style podcast. They can then swap roles and ask questions to another character. Students could produce their own news stories based on the novel that they have read. They can include audio descriptions of the characters and scenes along with interviews of multiple characters. It works best if they can find sound effects as well. This option takes more time but allows students to be fully immersed in the world of their novels.

Students might also do a TEDx-style talk in which they pretend to be a character, and they share what they have learned through the story. In other words, you might have Molly Weasley talk about death and knitting,[56] or Katniss could share what she knows about bowhunting and art.[57]

3. LEARNING JOURNEYS

Grades: 2-12

The teacher creates a set of reflective questions for students to use as they document their learning in an audio diary. They simply press record and share their thoughts in a stream of consciousness style. This works well in tandem with something like a design-thinking project. Here, students document what project they are working on and tell the story in the format of a narrative and reflection. They can focus each podcast episode on their goals, their process, their progress, and what they are learning along the way.

4. NARRATIVE-STYLE

Grades: 5-12

Students can engage in narrative-based podcasts by interviewing people and narrating the interview in a podcast style similar to something like *This American Life* or *Radiolab*.[58] This option requires additional time and resources for editing. You'll need to provide tutorials and perhaps even direct instruction to walk students through the process. However, it can be a great way to make current events relevant and help students make sense of informational texts and engage in meaningful journalism.

5. HISTORICAL FICTION

Grades: 4-8

Students can take on the role of people in another time period and create their own audio diaries, news stories, or question-and-answer shows. Students could do this with multiple voices and styles or in a style that is closer to that of an audiobook, where they read their historical short stories aloud. This can be simple and barely edited, or it can be complex and highly edited.

6. RANDOM OBJECTS PODCASTS

Grades: 6-12

We did this as a one-week unit in a way that was similar to the *50 Things That Made the Modern Economy.*[59] Here, students had to find random objects and tell the history of those particular objects. It was fascinating! We tied this to the standards of historical methods and research processes.

7. MATH IN REAL LIFE

Grades: 5-8

Students are challenged to find real-life applications for the math they are using. They can then describe their findings in a small-group podcast. As an extension, students can conduct interviews to see how people use math in their professions. This can work well with statistics and research, if you're teaching a more advanced math class.

VIDEO CREATION

Video creation is a little more complicated. They are often more time-consuming and sometimes require additional skills. However, if students are at home, they might just be willing to spend the additional time creating a video. A simple option for video creation is the annotated slideshow. Here, students create a slideshow and then record the audio as they move through it.[60]

A more advanced option is to create videos with their smartphones and then edit them on a computer. I've seen math teachers have students create videos explaining math concepts or sharing their processes for how to solve problems. I've seen science teachers encourage students to conduct an experiment at home and video record their process. In social studies, they might research a particular concept and then present their findings in a video.

Blogging, podcasting, and video creation are simple ways that students can create their own content. Students can also create infographics, make slideshows, or engage in digital modeling. However, at some point, we might expand student ownership of the creative process into a larger PBL unit.

PILOT A PBL UNIT

If you think about your most powerful learning experiences, there's a good chance at least one of these experiences involved a project. This is where you learned how to research, how to ideate, how to work with others, how to engage in productive struggle, and how to revise your work. These epic projects were what built those lifelong soft skills that you use on a regular basis.

I recently asked teachers to list the benefits they see in collaborative projects. Here are some of the things students learned:

- **Perseverance:** how to keep going even when a task is difficult
- **Project management:** how to plan, monitor, and assess projects
- **Communication:** how to communicate, resolve conflict, and show empathy toward others
- **Maker mindset:** how to define themselves as problem-solvers, designers, creators, and builders
- **Systems thinking:** how to navigate external systems
- **Ownership:** how to increase their sense of agency and develop their own voice
- **Critical thinking:** how to engage in analysis, evaluation, and the generation of new ideas in an authentic context

- **Adaptability:** how to become flexible thinkers
- **Inquiry:** how to ask great questions

This is why you might pilot a PBL unit. If you ask ten people to define PBL, you might get ten different answers. PBL isn't a learning theory. It's a pedagogical framework that incorporates elements of inquiry-based learning,[61] [62] [63] problem-based learning,[64] and service-learning.[65] On top of this, there isn't one single PBL process. However, while the specific frameworks vary, researchers agree on some key components that make up PBL:

- an initial question, scenario, or provocation[66]
- sustained inquiry[67]
- student-directed authentic research; each student is actively constructing knowledge through the project[68]
- student-generated ideas and products[69]
- shared work with an authentic audience[70]
- student engagement in reflection[71]
- an emphasis on self-direction and choice[72]

These PBL experiences typically take place in a physical environment, where students can collaborate together, and you, as the facilitator, can pull small groups and monitor project progress. But how do we do PBL in a distance learning environment? I want to point out ahead of time that there is no instruction manual for this. It will vary by grade level and content area. However, there are some big ideas that I would like to share.

If you walk into a PBL classroom, there's a good chance that you'll see movement and conversations. You might even see hands-on learning, with tools and physical materials. Now shift toward distance learning. Chances are, you'll see students working alone in front of a laptop or a tablet. However, distance learning doesn't have to mean spending hours in front of a screen. Students can still do hands-on prototyping and engage in movement as they work on projects at home. In many cases, the physical environment might even allow for more movement than a typical classroom, where you have a small space and tons of furniture. Here are a couple of ideas to make this happen:

- Schedule project time that will be on screen and off screen. In other words, you can meet your whole class for a virtual hang out where you do a class meeting and debrief project goals and progress (similar to a standing meeting) but then send them off to work on something physical and hands on.
- Ask students to find supplies and work within the creative constraint to design something new. Sometimes, masking tape and cardboard are the best options for boosting creative thinking. We used to do pinball-machine projects in which students brought in random items from home, along with cardboard and packing tape. You can take the same approach here by asking students to find items they can upcycle for their physical prototyping. Note that you need to be cognizant of equity here, and you might need to find ways to provide additional supplies for certain students. I've seen schools add project supplies and book checkouts to their daily free breakfast and free lunch programs.
- Have students do hands-on learning but also use their smartphone for synchronous communication. They can text, use video chat, or make phone calls. If they're younger, they might stay on a small group video conference. But the idea is that the communication tool is on in the background, giving a sense of proximity while the work is being done in a physical, hands-on way.
- You can create projects that blend together the lo-fi and the high-tech. In other words, they might do a physical prototype but video record the process. Students might sketch ideas out by hand but create a sketchnote video.

Larger PBL units can be time-consuming. If you have a tight curriculum map or a condensed schedule, you might choose shorter creative mini-projects instead. One idea is a design sprint.

LAUNCH A DESIGN SPRINT

A design sprint is a shorter mini-project that students can do in a single day or in a few hours. Unlike PBL, these mini-projects typically have less research and less ideation and more time in rapid prototyping. The goal is for students to get making as quickly as possible. The following is a prompt for a quick design sprint:

You need to design a sport that people can play together even when they are physically far apart. The goal is to create a high-interest game that requires physical movement. What is the goal of your sport? How will you win? Will you have points, or will it end when you reach a specific objective? Will it be timed? Will you have specific rounds? Will you take turns? How many players will you need? Will it be a team sport or an individual sport? Will your sport have positions? If so, what will each person do? What materials will you use? What items can you use from home? How will you blend together the physical environment with technology? What will the dimensions of the field or court be? Will you play it indoors or outdoors? Will it be loud or quiet? What will the rules be? What will you allow? What will be forbidden? What are the consequences for a penalty?

Now invent that sport. You must work collaboratively with two to four people at a distance using email, shared documents, chat, or video conferencing. Be sure to make your game inclusive so everyone can play. The goal is to create something that is both fun and active at the same time. Now go out and make something awesome!

With a design sprint, students develop their own plan of action. Unlike a larger PBL unit or a design-thinking project, students can decide how much time they devote to research, ideation, prototyping, and revision. The goal is for students to not only own the creative process but own the time management process as well. Other times, though, you might give students tight constraints, which can help spark creative thinking. One idea is a divergent thinking challenge.

DIVERGENT THINKING CHALLENGE

A divergent thinking challenge is similar to a design sprint, but it's built on the idea of creative constraint. With limited resources, students must then use items in new and unusual ways.[73]

Step 1: In a video conference, provide students with a divergent thinking prompt. One option is to create a scavenger hunt in which students find something fuzzy, something large, and something small. Or, they might find something sticky, something round, and something flat. After finding those items, they can then brainstorm all the things they can make with these items. This brainstorming phase is often hands-on. Students might work individually or in a breakout room in the video chat. Their brainstorms might be in the form of a list or in a web.

Step 2: Students analyze their ideas, combine any that seem similar, and scratch out any that they want to abandon. They might also mashup any unrelated ideas that might work well together.

Step 3: Students choose one main idea from the list and make a product with it. You might provide a specific time constraint to push their divergent thinking even more.

Step 4: Students go through multiple iterations until their product is done.

Step 5: Students create a video demonstrating how their product works and an explanation of their ideal audience.

EMPOWERING STUDENTS TO LAUNCH THEIR WORK

Students should have a voice in where they send their work. Part of owning the creative process is having the opportunity to clarify the audience and develop a strategy for reaching them. So, students might have blog posts that they share with their class-mates and others that they share with the entire world. You can think about audiences in layers:

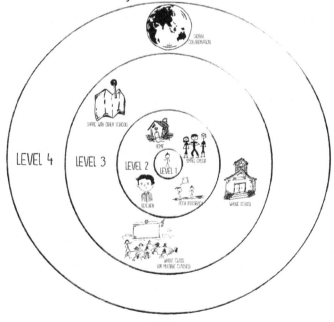

LEVEL 1: PRIVATE

Students reflect alone. Even the teacher doesn't get a chance to read their reflections and insights.

LEVEL 2: SEMI-PRIVATE

Students might share with their partners, small groups, or teacher. In some cases, the students might share their work with their family at home. For the most part, the sharing stays within the confines of the classroom walls (or, in this case, virtual classroom walls).

LEVEL 3: SEMI-PUBLIC

Students engage in multi-class collaboration (global projects), the whole school, or other classes within their school (other class periods). Although it's not totally public, the audience is still bigger than the immediate classroom.

LEVEL 4: PUBLIC

Students share with the world. This is riskier than other options. Students might face negative comments and trolling. Some parents and guardians will need their children to remain private due to safety or privacy issues at home. For this reason, it is critical that you have the correct permission forms and that you thoroughly explain privacy and consent with students and their families.

EMPOWER STUDENTS TO BE MAKERS

On a small level, we can incorporate creative thinking into all of our lessons. This happens any time we ask students to think divergently, generate ideas, or solve problems. However, we can go to the next level by doing a project or a mini-project. When this happens, we are affirming each student's identity and helping them develop their creative voice.

THEY EMBRACE
CONSTRUCTIVE
CRITICISM

THEY BECOME
FEARLESS

THEY GROW MORE
EMPATHETIC

THEY WORK
HARDER

WHY SHOULD STUDENTS
SHARE THEIR WORK
WITH AN AUDIENCE?

THEY DEVELOP A
GROWTH MINDSET

THEY ENGAGE
IN ITERATIVE
THINKING

THEY FIND THEIR
CREATIVE VOICE

THEY CONNECT
LEARNING TO
THEIR WORLD

CHAPTER 12

EMPOWERING TEAMS IN
COLLABORATIVE
WORK

We've all been there before when we were students. You'd hear the dreaded words "group project" and immediately begin calculating the additional work that you would need to do to keep the group afloat. You would check the list of names on the board. You'd be with the drifter, who wanders around the class chatting with friends. You would have the needy student who wants to ask the teacher a series of questions before making any decisions. Then you'd have the feisty fighter who picks arguments out of sheer boredom. At that point, you would realize that you'd be doing four times the amount of work you would normally do on a project.

It's no wonder that so few remote-learning classes include collaborative grouping. After all, the challenges of in-person groups seem amplified in virtual spaces. There tends to be less accountability for group members and less oversight from instructors. It is easier for students to disappear and avoid getting work done. Logistically, it can be challenging to schedule collaborative meetings. For this reason, it's tempting to avoid group work in distance learning and hybrid-learning courses.

And yet, remote learning often leads to isolation. During the pandemic, many students described the feelings of loneliness and disconnect as they shifted into online environments. We are social creatures, and we need human interaction. This disconnect is amplified when online courses are designed with only individual work in mind. As mentioned before, success in an online course depends on the relationship between the student and the content, the student and the instructor, and the student and classmates. Furthermore, when students are not collaborating with classmates, they miss out on new perspectives, new ideas, and new approaches to solving problems. They miss out on the opportunity to develop critical soft skills, such as communication, problem-solving, and creative thinking.

The key, then, is to craft learning experiences that can make the most out of collaboration. This is admittedly challenging. However, we can help students become better self-starters and self-managers in their small groups when we design structures to increase student ownership in the collaborative process.

ENSURE INDIVIDUAL ACCOUNTABILITY

Student ownership begins at the individual level. Although group members are working together as a whole, each individual member should be contributing. If students are working on a group project, they should move between individual, partner, and small-group tasks. This has the added bonus of allowing introverts additional processing time while also ensuring that each student is accountable for their own work.

It helps to start from a place of interdependent learning. If independent learning is fully autonomous and dependent learning involves students simply depending on another person, interdependence is the overlap, where students have autonomy, but they must have mutual dependence on one another. In other words, if one person fails to complete their work, every student struggles.

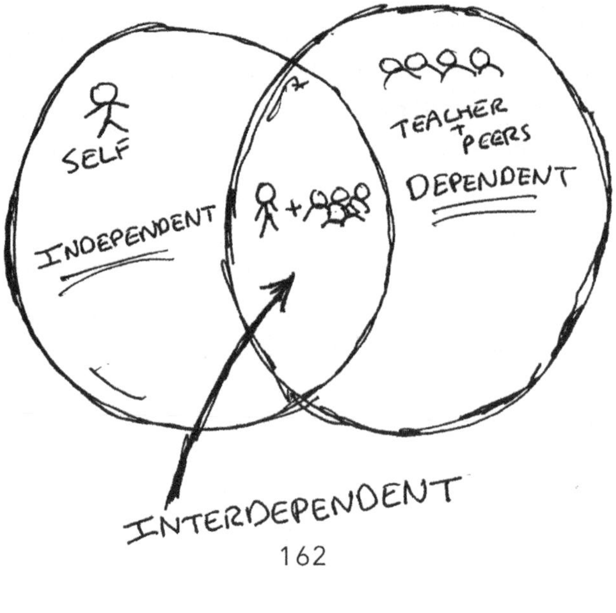

When students work interdependently, each member is adding value to the group project. One example is the interdependent brainstorming strategy. Here, each group member generates ideas alone, then meets together as a whole group to share, narrow down, and clarify ideas.

Notice that students must listen to one another and depend on each other for new ideas. At the same time, they each must each contribute to the process. There's an inherently low barrier of entry as well. Even the "low" student has something valuable to add to the group. This is a core idea of interdependence. Each member has something valuable to add to the process. A distance learning variation is to have students submit their ideas on a shared Google Form and then analyze the spreadsheet afterward. They can nego-tiate their ideas with a video chat or using a shared document.

Similarly, when doing research, every student can add additional information to the group's shared knowledge. They can read articles online or listen to podcasts independently of their group. Afterward, they each share what they learned during an interde-pendent research debrief. Students can share their information in a group chat or in a video conference. Or, they might simply add their ideas to a graphic organizer asynchronously through a shared document.

In some cases, you might assign roles that correspond to mastery levels. For example, when students move from inquiry to research, they often need to narrow down their questions to deter-mine which ones will actually guide the research process. Here's what the process looks like. See if you can spot the interdepend-ency and differentiation.

- Students generate questions independently. They might need sample questions or sentence stems, but they can all create questions individually. Once they have their questions, they can send them to a shared document or online form.

- Students meet up via video conference or on the phone to analyze the questions to see if they are actually research questions. Each member has a role. The first member checks to see if the question is fact-based. The second checks if it is on topic. The third checks to see if it is specific. The fourth person is the quality-control leader.
- Members 1-3 can put a star by each question that fits their criteria. So, member 1 looks at each question and puts a star by questions that are fact-based. Meanwhile, member 4 is available to help and observe. Then, member 4 double-checks all the questions with three stars and circles or highlights it if it's an actual research question.

Note that a struggling student might still be able to do the job of member 1 or 2, while a more advanced student can do member 3's job. Meanwhile, the group member who typically dominates and achieves at a higher academic level learns to trust other members and wait and observe. However, they can still provide expertise as the quality-control person who has the final say.

Interdependent structures will not guarantee that every student engages in collaborative work. Teams will often need to navigate conflict to deal with students who disengage. It's important to remember that disengagement is complicated. Some students check out because the task seems too hard or too confusing. Others struggle to get along with their teammates. For this reason, it helps to have team members develop a set of shared norms or expectations.

EMPOWER TEAMS TO SET NORMS AND EXPECTATIONS

While it is important to have student-generated norms for the entire class community, it's also important to have students develop norms as a team. As a teacher, you might suggest a few categories, such as responsibility, communication, active participation, conflict resolution, and respect. You might even ask students to look at sample norms.

Once groups have created an initial brainstorm of norms, place students in other groups to see if there are any norms from other groups that they may want to add. Next, have groups expand their norms and then narrow down their list of norms. Finally, they can wordsmith their norms. The goal should be consensus rather than voting. In other words, the norms should be agreed upon by every member of the team.

It's important that students understand that the norms are their shared expectations. When working in teams, they might need to remind themselves of the norms. Over time, though, these norms become an internalized part of the small-group's identity.

After developing norms, group members need a process to provide feedback to one another. Some teachers provide group contracts, so each team has the norms and consequences. Other teachers use mediation techniques to help students who are struggling to work together in teams. It often starts with a peer-mediation process. If that fails, the instructor can guide the conflict-resolution process. Another option is to use anonymous surveys in which each team member shares how the group is functioning in key areas such as communication, trust, conflict resolution, and productivity. Here, group members do not rate one another. Instead, they assess the team as a whole.

Note that having students grade one another can backfire. This can actually create risk aversion, where team members are afraid to speak up. It can also introduce an unhealthy power dynamic. Furthermore, students are not trained in assessment theory and practice. You, as the instructor, should be the sole person grading group members.

EMPOWER TEAMS TO OWN
THE PROJECT-MANAGEMENT PROCESS

Teams often struggle with self-management. They miss deadlines and fail to use their time effectively. Even when they have interdependent structures, and they have developed group norms, the entire small group can become unproductive throughout a collaborative project. This is especially true in virtual environments, where the instructor isn't constantly present to get students on task.

The counterintuitive solution is for students to own the project-management process. As students own the process, they develop the skills of collaborative self-management.

Project management begins with goal setting based on the big picture idea of what you want to accomplish.[74] Here, students need to have a clear sense of where they are going and what it will look like when they are finished. As a teacher, you can help walk them through the visualization process by modeling the thinking process. You might provide sentence frames or even exemplars the first time they think strategically about their goals. You might hold a virtual meeting in which you provide feedback on their goals and help them break down tasks. You might even need to give students an initial list of suggested deadlines at first and then help them clarify deadlines as they progress through a project.

Project management also involves breaking the project down into tasks and subtasks with clear deadlines. As a teacher, you can empower groups to set deadlines on their own. You might provide a graphic organizer that helps them visualize each part of a task, creating a bridge between the abstract ideas with the concrete actions. In this phase, teams develop a plan of action and select the tools and materials.

If you're working collaboratively, you often divide up roles and responsibilities. Students can negotiate who will do specific tasks and who will own specific responsibilities. This can help ensure that groups are valuing individual student agency while also working as a cohesive team. As a teacher, you might create group roles as an initial framework and then allow team members to modify those roles as they see fit.

Next, students choose and implement specific strategies. Here, student ownership includes choosing their method of tracking progress. Some students might use a color-coded spreadsheet with tasks, subtasks, members responsible, and deadlines.

Or, they might use an online project management software, which can enable them to use progress bars, to-do lists, and virtual cards. Regardless of what students choose, the key is that they are choosing their ideal strategy for tracking their project progress.

Students will likely run into barriers, which will force them to problem-solve and experiment. They might even need to pivot and re-examine their original goals. But that is a chance for you, as a teacher, to walk them through the iterative process. When students learn the project-management process, they grow into self-directed learners, capable of being self-starters and self-managers.

EMPOWER TEAMS TO OWN
THE COMMUNICATION PROCESS

Sometimes, students struggle with collaboration in remote learning because of the challenges in virtual communication. It helps to teach students when to use both synchronous and asynchronous communication tools. In other words, you can empower groups to select the mode of communication and the apps they will use as they plan out their projects and set up their schedules. This can be a complicated process, and you might need to work with teams early on in their collaborative work to help clarify the communication process.

In collaborative work, synchronous communication is faster and more dynamic. It's great for active participation and interactive discussions. It tends to work well with smaller groups, which means students will likely use video chats and audio conversations as they work together. These synchronous tools can help students problem-solve in the moment and can help team members give one another quick feedback on their work. When all students are working virtually, they might choose to have the whole group on speakerphone or video so they can easily give one another instructions.

However, synchronous communication can lead to frequent interruptions and distractions that get in the way of deep work. It can also be harder for small groups to create a shared schedule in which all students can communicate synchronously at the same time.

Asynchronous communication works well when internet connection is unstable or when participants don't have shared schedules. It also tends to allow for a permanent record of the communication, which can be helpful with long-term projects. In addition, as students divide up tasks, they will often use asynchronous tools to share their creative work with one another.

Some platforms blend synchronous and asynchronous communication. A walkie-talkie app lets you communicate in the moment but also listen later and even adjust the speed. A shared document has real-time edits, but the comments are asynchronous, and there is a permanent record of all annotations. Video chats can occur in real-time but also be recorded for replay. Teams can leverage these blended synchronous-asynchronous tools to provide both flexibility and interactivity. Often, a group will use a walkie-talkie app or a chat with a default of communicating in the moment while allowing for flexibility with schedules. In some cases, though, you might have to help them navigate this terrain. This is why it's important to still check up on small groups.

EMPOWERED TEAMS STILL NEED CHECK-INS

Distance learning doesn't mean we have to be relationally distant. As teachers, we can be intentional about creating a sense of presence with our students. Here are a few ideas you might consider as you connect with small groups during collaborative work:

- **Small-group check-ins:** Here, you can schedule small-group meetings and use video conferencing to meet with groups and look at their progress. You can ask students about their challenges and help teams navigate conflict. You might ask them to reflect on their goals and their progress.

- **Email check-ups:** This idea is simple. Just send an email reminding students of the deadlines, but then ask them to respond to a reflective question. If they don't respond, it becomes a chance to reach out to them again.
- **Short text check-ins:** With this option, you can ask students to use the chat function to send questions or comments as you go. The key here is frequency.
- **Surveys:** Ask students to fill out a course survey each day where they share what their experiences have been in an online course. You can include specific surveys about how the group is functioning as a whole.

It's not always easy to make collaboration work in remote learning. In fact, it's rarely easy. Even when you design the systems well, challenges and conflicts will arise. Human interactions are inherently messy. However, the fact that it's challenging shouldn't discourage us from designing systems that boost creative collaboration. If anything, this points to a need for more collaborative work. We can design meaningful collaboration to help students develop soft skills they will use forever as they work in teams. Ultimately, it will be an experiment. Some things won't work. And that's okay. But when things do work, your students will be developing skills that last for a lifetime.

CHAPTER 13

EMPOWERING STUDENTS TO OWN THE
ASSESSMENT PROCESS

Assessment is all around us. If you're a skater at a skatepark, you're engaging in self-assessment every time you reflect on your progress and plan the next steps. If you're a runner training for a marathon, you look at time splits and compare it to your goals. If you're a musician, you're engaging in assessment every time you listen to yourself play and make modifications to your approach. As an author, you engage in self-assessment when you revise your work. It's not always individual.

Often, assessment happens in community. If you're a chef, you're engaging in peer assessment when you ask a trusted fellow chef, "How does this taste?" If you're an artist, you might ask for an extra set of eyes on a particular project. If you're an engineer, you might observe users to see if your design is working. If you do any kind of creative work, both self-assessment and peer assessment are vital for improving your craft. It helps you refine your process and helps you improve your products.

Assessment helps us figure how what we know, what we don't know, and what steps we need to take in the future to master a skill or understand a concept at a deeper level. This is true in life but also in the classroom. We often think of classroom assessment as a conversation between teachers and students. But in life, students won't always have a teacher to grade their work or provide them with necessary feedback. This is why we need self-assessment and peer assessment. The more we can integrate this into our lessons, the better prepared our students will be for the creative life.

STUDENT-CENTERED ASSESSMENT BOOSTS METACOGNITION

When students own the assessment process, they are able to figure out the following:

- what they already know (prior knowledge)
- what they don't know (areas of improvement)

- what they want to master (their goals)
- what they will do to improve (action plan)

As students improve in their metacognition, they grow into self-directed learners.[75] Over time, this process feels invisible. They hardly notice how often they are assessing tasks, determining their strengths, planning approaches, committing to an action, and monitoring their progress. In order to do this, though, they need to engage in frequent self-assessment.

SELF-ASSESSMENT

Self-assessments have an empowering effect. Instead of attributing academic success to a teacher or to luck, they see it as a result of their hard work. They grow more self-directed because they're frequently examining their own progress. The following are some self-assessment options:

- **Tracking goals:** Here students create specific learning goals and then track their progress over time. Students can keep track of their goals using online forms (such as Google Forms).
- **Self-reflections:** Students might reflect on their progress toward learning a new skill or concept. Other times, they might reflect on the learning process or reflect on their specific products. Students can write these self-reflections in a document, or they can create audio or video reflections.
- **Student surveys:** Unlike a self-reflection, student surveys allow students to answer multiple-choice questions, Likert scales, or checkboxes. This can be valuable for gathering trends over time for individual students and for gathering

whole-class data on something that is fairly subjective (student opinions). Students can access these online surveys through an email or within the course LMS.

- **Self-assessment rubrics:** We often use rubrics at the end of an assignment or project. We might even preview it ahead of time. However, there is value in having students use rubrics as a self-assessment tool in the moment. While there are many online rubric makers, you might simply use a shared document.

- **Checklists:** Checklists work great as a diagnostic tool for self-assessment. This can work for a specific skill (a checklist for writing a paragraph) or for a larger project. Students might generate checklists on their own or as a whole class. Other times, the teacher might share a checklist that the students use. You might also have students look at a rubric and convert the categories into checklists.

- **Concept maps:** A concept map (or mindmap) is a powerful way for students to show how concepts are connected. They can draw lines between ideas and choose color schemes, shapes, and sizes to represent contrasting ideas, organizational structures, or the importance of ideas. Unlike a web, which is typically a spoke and wheel, a true concept map doesn't have a center so much as a connection of lines between various ideas. In traditional assessments, we tend to focus on what students don't know. Think of a checkmark on a multiple-choice test. But with a concept map, students get to share what they do know. There are many great online concept map programs, but students might actually choose to draw their maps by hand and take a snapshot with their smartphones. They can then post their pictures directly to the class LMS.

- **Infographics:** An infographic is a visual representation of information. Often, it will include graphs, statistics, and a visualization of ideas.
- **Comparing to exemplars:** Students look at their work, compare it to an exemplar, and then reflect on their work. This is often what we do in life. We work on a project, and we compare it to examples that we see around us.
- **Portfolios:** With portfolios, students share their work and reflect on how they are doing. They might select works that demonstrate personal growth, or they might select work that demonstrates mastery. Their portfolios could be online with written or audio reflections, or they could be physical and tactile.

DIGITAL PORTFOLIO PROJECT

Premise:

For this type of portfolio, I encourage students to think about the product and the process through a lens of growth and mastery. Students also look at what they learned along the way and what future steps they want to take.

Time Frame:

I have found that three to five class periods tend to work well. I prefer taking a whole week if it is a yearlong class and taking three days (combining page 1 with 4 and 5, see below) for a semester-long course.

Technology Platform:

Students can create this on an online website creator or a blog. However, they could also take these same components and create video portfolios.

Page 1: Home

The goal of a home page is to introduce who you are, along with the purpose of the portfolio. The following are a few things you might want to include:

- a photo or snippet of one of your works
- a short description of who you are, including a few of your interests
- a list of skills you have gained in this field or subject
- a description of the purpose of the portfolio (showing your growth and your best work)
- a short description of your learning journey (What projects did you do? Who did you work with?)

Page 2: Growth

Begin with an introduction sharing how you have grown from the start of the course to the end of the course. Afterward, select at least two before and after examples (a total of four). The following questions might help guide you:

- Why does this newer work represent an area of growth for you? Cite specific examples of how you have improved.
- What were the hardest areas for you to master and why?
- In general, how has your work changed from start to finish?
- What obstacles did you face? How did you get past those obstacles? How did you grow as a result of facing those obstacles?
- Which standard or standards does this work connect to? In what ways does it prove you grew in this standard?

Page 3: Best Work

Begin an introduction sharing what part of this course or subject you are currently excelling in. Afterward, select your top three examples of your best work. The following questions might help guide you:

- Why is this an example of your best work?
- What aspects of this work make you feel proud? What makes this work stand out?
- Which standard or standards does this work connect to? In what ways does it prove you are exceeding the standard?
- Did you find this work to be easy or hard to do? Why is that?
- What skills did you use in order to create this? In what ways can you build on these skills in the future?
- What strengths or skills did you discover about yourself?

Page 4: What I Learned

Begin with an introduction to some of the basic skills you have learned. If possible, cite specific standards and your level of mastery. The following questions might help you along the way:

- What problems did you solve along the way?
- What skills have you learned? How can you apply these to other subjects?
- What concepts did you figure out?
- How did you contribute to group projects? What were your roles? What collaborative skills did you learn along the way?
- What did you learn about yourself in the process?

Page 5: Next Steps

Share what you plan to do next. The following questions might help you along the way:

- What are some areas that are still weaknesses for you? What will you do to continue to grow in these areas?
- What future goals do you have connected to this subject or topic? List the goals and keep them specific.
- How do you plan to use this in life? Cite actual examples.

WHEN STUDENTS DOCUMENT THEIR PROGRESS

In a physical classroom, teachers are constantly assessing through the simple act of observation. However, this is a challenge in remote learning. As an educator, it can feel as though you are removed from the process, only able to give feedback on finished works or on early drafts of assignments. This is why it helps to have students share their process along with their finished work. Here, students might share any of the following:

- what processes they are using to solve problems
- what skills they are learning
- what concepts they are learning and what misconceptions or area of confusion they are still experiencing
- what specifically they are creating and where they are in the design process
- what challenges they are facing and how they are persevering
- how they are feeling about their work, their abilities, and their motivational levels

Students can document their process with an ongoing form. Each day, they can fill out a few quick questions and then see their progress from day to day. If you use quantitative questions (on a scale of 1-5 how motivated are you), then students can track their own progress. For example, students might do a daily reading fluency exercise and rate their accuracy, pace, and expression using Google Forms.[76]

Another option is to have students create audio or video reflections on their learning process. In some cases, students might not feel like writing lengthy reflections. However, they are happy to press the record button and give a quick audio reflection on their process. Or, they might video record a section of their work and speed it up so that you can do a direct observation. You might even do a synchronous video chat and ask students to demonstrate a specific skill (which can be helpful in art, music, PE, or any other performance-based class).

PEER ASSESSMENT

With peer assessment, students provide meaningful feedback to one another throughout their learning. They might provide feedback on a specific work (an essay), or they might offer feedback on a process (how to solve an equation). In some cases, students meet as pairs to offer feedback in a workshop style. Other times, a single member meets with a small group. Still other times, one group might offer feedback for another group.

However, as mentioned earlier, it is critical that peer assessment does not become peer grading. You are the teacher and the expert on the content. While students can benefit from peer feedback, you ultimately know their level of mastery best. Also, peer grading can create unnecessary power dynamics that actually get in the way of meaningful feedback. Consider the role of peer reviews in companies. While most employees enjoy asking for feedback on a specific idea, they hate peer reviews – the biggest reason being that they feel judged and graded by their peers. If that's the case for adults, we want to avoid that dynamic with students.[77] Here are a few ways to do peer assessment

- **The twenty-minute peer feedback system:** This system is a highly structured ten-minute process in which each person pitches an idea or shows a product, followed by clarifying questions, feedback, and next steps. Afterward, the partners switch roles, thus taking twenty minutes total. This works best as a structure within a video chat.

- **Structured feedback with sentence stems:** Here, you provide specific sentence stems that your students can use to provide diagnostic, clarifying, or critical feedback. This type of feedback works well as a blog comment or as a form of feedback within a shared document.

- **3-2-1 structure:** This is simple. Students provide three strengths, two areas of improvement and one question that they have. Students can use this structure in both synchronous and asynchronous communication.

- **See-Think-Wonder:** Students give peer feedback by pointing out what they see in another product, what they think about it, and, finally, what questions they have. This tends to work well asynchronously as comments on a shared document or slideshow. Students can also post their work in an online forum and classmates can use this structure in the comment section below the artifact.[78]

- **Feedback carousel:** In the in-person version, each group gets a stack of sticky notes and offers anonymous feedback as they move from group to group. Unlike the other feedback methods, students here are offering feedback without the original group member present. It also focuses almost entirely on the product. If you're going digital, students can post their work on the LMS and leave comments below, or they can view videos in links and leave feedbacks with online sticky notes.[79]

- **Peer coaching:** Students interview each other about the process, using the coaching questions from the student-teacher conferences to guide them if they struggle to come up with reflection questions. This works well in a synchronous video call between students. You might have a larger class meeting and then break students up into pairs using the breakout room feature of your video chat. Students might even choose between peer coaching (open-ended) or the twenty-minute peer-feedback system.

- **Video feedback:** Students can use screencast videos to provide meaningful, conversational feedback on their classmates' work. With screencast videos, students can hear the tone of voice in their feedback, and they can explain things in the moment. However, unlike synchronous peer coaching, students can watch this feedback at any time.

- **Mastermind:** In a mastermind group, members meet together on a regular basis and share their work, their goals, their progress, and their ideas. Each member has a timed "sweet seat" in which they share and listen to feedback from others. Unlike the ten-minute feedback system, the "sweet seat" is less structured and is directed by the person in the sweet seat. In other words, I might say, "This is my idea and I want feedback," or I might say, "I'm looking for ideas on . . ." It's up to me, in the sweet seat, to direct this time.

TRUST IS VITAL

Sometimes students struggle with peer feedback. For this reason, I created the trust-feedback grid. When the feedback is positive but there is negative trust, you end up with flattery. This feels great but it's potentially toxic and often manipulative. When there's distrust and negative feedback, it's just hating. When the feedback is negative but there's a high level of trust, you actually have critical feedback. It doesn't feel good but it's often where growth happens. Finally, when the feedback is positive and there's a high level of trust, you have affirmation – and we all need more affirmation in our lives. These are the words that can pull you through even when you stop believing in yourself. Note that trust levels can change over time with personal growth, relational dynamics, and events. Also, trust is often task-specific and context-specific.

TRUST AND FEEDBACK GRID

Students sometimes struggle with giving and receiving critical feedback. This is why I created the trust and feedback grid.

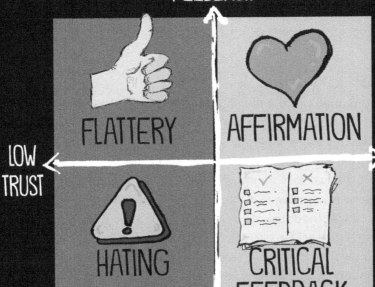

POSITIVE
FEEDBACK

FLATTERY

AFFIRMATION

LOW
TRUST

HIGH
TRUST

HATING

CRITICAL
FEEDBACK

NEGATIVE
FEEDBACK

STUDENT MASTERMIND GROUPS

Let's take a deeper dive into mastermind groups. The following are a few of the things you might do as you meet with your mastermind group:

- Share your journey with the group and let them hear what you are learning along the way.
- Share your needs with others and ask for ideas or resources.
- Share your frustrations (there's a power to being vulnerable).
- Share your success stories and celebrate success together.
- Talk about potential collaboration options together.

Student mastermind groups work well when engaged in long-term projects. However, they can also function as a way to focus on the learning process and to share learning goals. For example, undergraduate science students might meet together to share goals and to review their progress within the program. Meanwhile, students in a fifth-grade class might use the mastermind structure to review their reading goals.

The following is the mastermind "sweet seat" format (other groups call this the "hot seat") that I used when I was working on my doctorate. My advisor first introduced us to this, and I've since used it with other mastermind groups as well. I have modified the structure since then, and I'd like to share it with you.

Roles
- Facilitator: guides the process
- Timekeeper: keeps everyone on track with time deadlines
- Scribe: keeps track of goals

Part 1: Introductions

The facilitator opens the group up by reviewing the group norms and the mastermind sweet seat process. This might also be when people volunteer to go first, second, third, etc. Note that a mastermind group should be limited to no more than six people.

Part 2: Opening Round

The facilitator asks each person to complete the following:

- At this moment, I am feeling _____ about _____.
- My "big win" for the past week was _____.
- Regarding my former commitments, I _____.
- One key challenge I'm dealing with is _____.
- With regards to my goals, I am _____.

Part 3: Sweet Seat

The timekeeper sets a timer for ten minutes. It helps to have someone who is bold and even ruthless with time management to keep people on track.

The sweet seat begins with the student discussing how they're doing on their project. They might share challenges and experiences and even ask for support. In some cases, they might have a specific idea, and they want feedback from the mastermind group. Afterward, the rest of the mastermind group provides feedback and shares ideas.

When the timer goes off, it's the next person's turn. We have a rule that nobody is allowed to interrupt the person during the sweet seat time. Instead, this person in the sweet seat invites feedback by asking a question of saying, "I'd like feedback, please." This can help honor student agency and prevent students from feeling attacked.

Part 4: Closing Round

The facilitator asks each person to complete the following, for a total of ten minutes:

- My "big takeaway" from this meeting is _____.
- This week I commit to _____.
- My big goal is to _____.
- This next week, I would like to try _____.

The scribe writes these down in a safe place. In some cases, the scribe might do a follow-up email as a reminder to fellow team members.

Optional Scheduling: Review the next meeting time, assign facilitator, scribe, and timekeeper roles.

This format can be empowering because they learn how to ask for help while also provide support for others. There's a power in the proximity and the vulnerability of a mastermind group. Creative work can be frustrating and even scary at times. Distance learning can feel isolating. However, students share their goals, hopes, and struggles, and they learn they're not alone.

TEACHER ASSESSMENT

Although student ownership is critical to assessment, teachers still play a vital role in the assessment process. One of my favorite methods is through student-teacher conferences. The concept is simple. Plan out three to four mini-conferences per class period. Each conference lasts about five minutes. This generally allows you to meet with each student individually once every two weeks. In a PBL unit, you spend less time in direct instruction and guided practice, which frees you up to have richer feedback conversations with students. This is especially true in virtual environments. The following are the four types of conferences I have used with students:

- **Advice conference**: Students ask teachers specific questions that the teacher answers. In some cases, this might be a short tutoring session. Other times, it could be overall advice on a specific project. When every student does an advice conference, it sends the message that we are all learners, and we are all in need of help.
- **Reflection conferences**: Unlike the advice conferences, the reflection conferences begin with the teacher asking students questions. This helps students as they reflect on their learning. Some of these are more academic, while others are more social-emotional.
- **Mastery conference:** The student and the teacher sit together and discuss the student's mastery toward a particular standard. This helps students figure out where they are and where they need to be. At the end, students then set goals.
- **Pulse check:** This is an informal conference in which the teacher simply checks in to see how a student is doing. This is the most open-ended of the conferences and does not require a particular protocol. These are ideal when a student is suddenly missing work or seeming to struggle. However, they can also be helpful in general just to see how students are doing. Students might talk about how they feel about the class and the subject or their group members.

As a teacher, you can ask students to self-select the type of conferences they prefer before having a video conference or an in-class meeting.

THE CHANGING ROLE OF THE TEACHER

When teachers embrace peer assessment and self-assessment, it changes the role of the teacher in assessment. Instead of being the sole source of feedback, you become the facilitator of feedback within the classroom community. This can then free you up to spend more time giving quality feedback and less time grading papers. While it might seem like a less significant role, you actually have a greater role in the assessment process because you are teaching students how to engage in authentic assessment at an individual and peer level.

CHAPTER 14

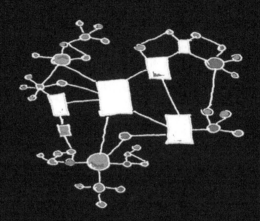

DESIGNING SYSTEMS FOR
STUDENT
EMPOWERMENT

Five years ago, I opened my first ever online course evaluation as a professor. Initially, the scores were positive with a 4.7 and 4.9 out of 5 points. Students found the course materials enjoyable and relevant. They loved having voice and choice in their projects. I felt pretty good about the course until I zeroed in on the 1.9 in course organization and the 1.6 in communicating expectations. I also earned a 2.9 in overall communication.

How could this be right? I communicated often with students. I left meaningful comments on their work. I posted a weekly video to our LMS. I even sent individual emails to students reminding them to turn in their late work.

Then, I read the comments. Students described feeling overwhelmed by the sheer number of course resources and the feeling frustrated that nothing was housed in the same place. One student described the challenge of figuring out if a "class discussion" was on the asynchronous forum or the weekly video chat. Another student mentioned turning an assignment in late because it wasn't listed in the course calendar but was included in the weekly module as a class activity.

This course evaluation shook me to the core. As a middle-school teacher, I knew how to create seamless organization systems. I had conducted a professional development module for new teachers on how to manage the paper trail and how to stay organized. However, online my course was a mess. I had spent twelve years creating consistent templates for slideshows and assignments for my middle schoolers, but in this online course, I had failed to use consistent formatting and language in our materials and assignments. As a middle-school teacher, I would conduct student surveys and ask for frequent feedback to refine my course materials, but I failed to do so in this online course.

The next day, I met with my friend Luke Neff, an expert in systems thinking and a current technology director. He was also one of our strongest adjunct professors. Students had specifically mentioned how well-designed his courses were.

Luke listened to my story, which began with a defensive and frustrated tone. Then, he said something that stuck with me. "I've always told myself that I never want to be surprised by course evaluations." He then described specific ways he sought out feedback throughout the course so that he could modify the design and make it more student-friendly.

This notion of student feedback was a core idea of UX design theory.[80] Together, we talked through specific ways to use UX design principals in my next online course. I put all of my course assignment directions into a single Google Document with internal bookmarks. I created a plan for student feedback, starting with having students annotate the course documents and continuing with continual surveys. I crafted an onboarding video previewing the course. The next semester, students rated my course a 4.7 in organization.

One student described how the use of the surveys actually helped them feel more known on a personal level. In the previous chapters, we explored specific ways we can empower students to own their learning in hybrid and remote learning spaces. However, sometimes students disengage because a course has poorly designed systems. If students struggle to navigate a course, it creates an additional hurdle to access the learning. A teacher might do a great job communicating with students and building a classroom community, but if the systems for communication breakdown, it impacts the relationships within the community.

In this chapter, we explore how instructors can create better course systems and structures using the principles of UX design theory. When courses have a seamless, intuitive feel, students can focus on their learning. The goal is to reduce cognitive load (how hard they are thinking about a task) in task analysis so students can spend more mental energy on their learning.

THE POWER OF UX DESIGN

When I was a kid, nothing had wheels. Trash night was an athletic endeavor. We had to haul trash cans down our long country driveway because they didn't have wheels. Similarly, we had to lug our luggage across the airport because, again, no wheels. I'm not entirely sure why, but it took well over a century for people to say, "This is an unpleasant experience. Maybe we should use wheels."

We hardly think about luggage until we buy one that tips over too easily or has wheels that get stuck. Similarly, we rarely think about smartphone design until you can't navigate a particular app. This is because great design is like a ninja. It's powerful and effective, but you don't really see it. It's so intuitive that you hardly pay attention to it. However, bad design is noticeable. Consider the example of stoves. In my last house, the stovetop had a straight horizontal row of nobs that corresponded to the four burners. It took months to remember which nob fit which burner. Years later when I was cooking dinner, the knobs would still trip me up. By contrast, my current stove has a matching set of knobs that correspond to the burner in the exact same pattern. I don't even think about which knob to use. It just works.

This idea is at the heart of UX design theory (sometimes abbreviated as XD, UX, UXD, or UED), as it focuses on the user experience of a system or product. This might include accessibility, usability, enjoyment, and the overall flow of the experience. UX design focuses on systems in a way that is deeply human. What does it feel like for people? What does it look like for them? What are their processes? How do they interact with it?

UX design aims to build systems that people will intuitively understand rather than trying to get people to fit into a system. When the UX design works in my classroom, students hardly notice it. This frees them up to focus on the learning tasks at hand. However, when the UX design is bad, they get frustrated with me and often end up confused with the learning tasks. They have a harder time focusing because nothing feels intuitive. Quality UX design decreases cognitive load (or the overall amount of thinking going) so that students can focus on deeper learning. It also saves time because you spend less class time going over procedures and directions. In general, UX design focuses on the following areas:

- **Onboarding:** There is a solid preview of how things work. It can be simple. When you go to a restaurant, there is likely a sign that reads, "Please seat yourself," or "Please wait to be seated." This is an onboarding experience alerting you to how the restaurant works. In a classroom, onboarding might be a course preview video or a set of visual cues.
- **User feedback**: UX design stresses the role of user feedback by observing people or asking for their feedback. This helps designers tweak and improve the systems. In a classroom, this means there are opportunities to observe students and ask for their feedback on the materials and systems.
- **Intuitive design:** There is a sense that you know exactly what you need to do. You are able to figure it out naturally.
- **Consistency in language:** The language remains the same in each place and in every occurrence that it's used. Think about Facebook. A group is always a group. A page is always a page. However, in classrooms, we often use many phrases interchangeably. A group is also a small group is also a team. An essay is also a paper. On some level, this is normal. Students need to learn that words can be used interchangeably. However, sometimes the multiple terms cause confusion.
- **Consistency in experience:** I have the newest version of iPhone and the experience is slightly different from the original

experience. However, I generally know that I will sweep and hit tiles to view apps. This is a consistent experience. In a classroom, we can use a consistent template used for lessons or materials and for physical systems. This helps create stability for students as they walk in each day.

- **Simplicity:** Great UX design is simple, even when the context is complicated.
- **Universal design:** Everyone should be able to access the system. Think of closed captioning on television or voice to text on a phone. The system or material is fully accessible to all students. We explored this idea previously in our chapter on equity and access. However, it's important that we include this same focus on our systems design as well.

USING UX DESIGN TO TRANSFORM YOUR SYSTEMS

As an instructor, you are constantly designing systems. These might be the organizational systems, the learning systems, or the materials you use in your courses. With UX design, you can craft systems that are logical, intuitive, and easy to navigate. Here are seven ideas of UX design that I am trying to incorporate into my course design.[81]

1. EMBRACE ONBOARDING.

Sign up for a website and you'll probably experience a "virtual tour." Often, it's something simple, with things clearly labeled as you use them. They might have pop-ups or rollover text or part of the screen that gets lighter. Platform designers want you to feel comfortable as you easily navigate that first experience.

Similarly, we can use an onboarding approach with our remote and hybrid courses. You might include a "start here" section in your LMS with a video tour of the course. The goal of an onboarding experience is to alleviate fear, help students feel comfortable, and answer questions as you go rather than giving a list of instructions ahead of time.

A few years ago, I split-tested two onboarding video approaches. In the first video, I created a traditional instructional video. I explained how the assignments worked in a logical, sequential way, answering questions that I thought students might ask. In the second video, I created an "unboxing" video, where I took on the role of a student. I said, "I want you to pretend I'm a student. So, here's what I'm seeing. Here's what I think I'll do. Next, I'm going to want to . . ." Students overwhelmingly chose the second "unboxing" approach rather than the traditional instructional approach because it was focused on the initial experience.

When teaching classes in person, you can do a preview exploration of your classroom. Or, if you want to add a gaming element to it, you can do unboxing through an escape-room activity that allows students to explore the classroom space through small challenges that unlock the next element.

While we tend to think of onboarding as a process for the start of a course, we can apply this same principle to the beginning of the week. Teachers and professors can create a short video preview explaining the week's assignments, discussions, materials, and themes. In some cases, instructors might even put together an entire course online and allow students to access the materials and assignments for upcoming weeks.

2. BEGIN WITH THE STUDENTS IN MIND.

User experience should focus on making processes easier for the students to navigate. As the instructor, you might collect surveys and needs assessments to help you focus on how to improve the student experience. When teaching in person, you can take notes on the "pain points" you notice from activities that didn't flow well. Where are students getting confused? What needs to be modified? How can this process be more intuitive?

As you begin designing a course or planning a lesson, you can picture the experience from the perspective of a student. You might even close your eyes and visualize what it's like to be a student in your class on the first day. This visualization exercise can help frame the design process through a lens of empathy.

Later, you can ask students about their experience. You might have students complete a survey or simply email you a quick response about what it felt like to navigate your course online or in person. You can then use that feedback to continue to iterate in your course design.

3. BE INTENTIONAL WITH COPY TEXT.

If you check out the sites you frequent most often, they have clear, easy-to-understand copy text. It's why you can hop on YouTube and figure out within seconds where you need to go. This copy text feels invisible. Most of the time, you don't even notice it. But that's the point. This invisible design is what makes it work so well.

How can we create short, simple text that guides students intuitively through systems? How do we create simple, minimalist visuals that accomplish the same thing? What would it mean to create instructions with clarity and brevity rather than attempting to be comprehensive? Here are a few ideas:

- **Use shorter sentences with clear action verbs.** If you're curious what this looks like, pay attention to real-world examples of instructions. This could be instruction manuals or recipe books, but it might also be the text you see on road signs, in restaurants, or on social media apps. Take note of how simple the phrases are and how rarely they use adjectives or adverbs.
- **Split test phrases.** Try two different sets of directions and ask students to select which phrase is easier to understand. You don't need to do this frequently, but on occasion, you might have two sets of directions and ask students, "Which one works better for you?"
- **Make use of headings and subheadings.** Also, use bold and italic fonts for visual cues. In some cases, you might even create additional view cues in brackets, such as [URGENT] or [NEW].
- **Use an active voice.** Directions are often written in passive voice (just like this sentence). However, when you write

directions in a clear, active voice, students feel more of a sense of urgency with learning tasks.

- **Use second-person language.** In other words, rather than writing, "The students will . . ." or "The teams need to . . ." use "You will . . ." and "Your team needs to . . ." This might seem subtle, but the second-person phrasing conveys a greater sense of urgency with a tone that is more direct than it would be in third person.

These examples might seem hyper-specific, but sometimes small tweaks in language can have a great impact on students. You don't need to obsess over the language or spend too much time rewriting instructions. However, we can get into a mindset where we approach copy text with a sense of intentionality.

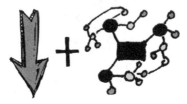

4. BE LINEAR BUT BE CONNECTIVE.

Open any well-designed app on your phone and you'll notice a logical, linear flow. Things are exactly where they need to be. You can go sequentially through things, and you won't feel lost. At the same time, there's a good chance that you can move back and forth between things at any time. This is part of what makes the user experience work. It's the notion of being logical but intuitive and being linear but also connective.

When we think about course design, we need to consider how things can flow logically and sequentially in a linear way. At the same time, we need to incorporate elements of a web-like, connective experience. For example, when creating a course calendar, you can put all of the assignment directions on one shared document. At the top of the document, you can have a course calendar with the week, the assignments due, and the assignments given.

You might also link to course materials. Below the course calendar, you can then add the detailed assignment directions. If there is a corresponding handout, simply create a clear "download this assignment" link within the directions.

At this point, the document is a long, linear, logical description of the course. However, you can then add internal bookmarks for each assignment and hyperlink those to the course calendar. Suddenly, the shared document is both linear and connective. It becomes a one-stop place for all course materials.

5. BE CONSISTENT.

If you go on Twitter, you'll notice that a profile is always called a profile. Notifications are always referred to as notifications and never alerts or messages. The explore option is always explore and never "find" or "search." The search function is always its own entity. The symbols remain constant and always correspond to the tasks. These simple flat design icons remain consistent throughout the platform. The framework and interface stay the same. When Twitter does an update, people freak out! For a day. Then they get over it because even after an update, the language remains consistent and the icons remain largely intact. That's the beauty of consistent design. It's the idea of using patterns and familiarity to speed up cognition so that students can focus on what they are learning.

I'm not suggesting that we do the exact same thing in a class-room. It would feel weird to standardize the language. We're humans, and we need to use synonyms. So, we can use the terms "conversations" and "discussions" interchangeably.

However, there is value in incorporating consistent language and predictable frameworks so that students know what to expect in online and hybrid courses.

For example, in my online courses, I always use the term "small group" rather than "team." I use the term "weekly discussions" rather than "forums" or "conversations." This might not seem like a big deal but it allows students to move seamlessly through a course without needing to rethink what a term might mean. Our small-group discussions happen virtually in breakout rooms. Similarly, I use consistent language with assignments and projects. I use the term "professional educator blogs" rather than "teacher blogs" or even "educator blogs." Each time I use this term online, I hyperlink the text to go back to the assignment directions.

This is also why I use the same templates each time I write assignment directions. I continually use student feedback to guide future revisions. I want the handouts to be clear, concise, intentional, and intuitive. You can check out the format below.

Assignment Name

OVERVIEW
Describe the assignment with a rationale.

GROUPING
Explain the grouping.

DIRECTIONS
Provide step-by-step directions.

HANDOUTS

After reading the directions, students can access any relevant handouts. I also include links to any relevant tutorials they might need to access.

EXAMPLES
While this isn't always necessary, there are times I might add an exemplar that students can access.

ASSIGNMENT FORMAT
Explain the format for the assignment (video, audio, etc.).

SUBMITTING THE ASSIGNMENT
Provide specific directions on how to submit, including links to things like Google Classroom submissions, how to zip a file, posting a link, and so on.

GRADING
I include the grading process, the point value, and the rubric or checklist students will use.

DUE DATE
Clearly provide the date that it is due.

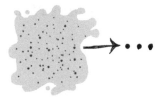

6. BE SIMPLE.

Open the Instagram app, and you'll see a home icon, a search icon, the picture icon, the heart icon, and the profile icon. You have five simple icons with no words. But packed within each icon is a ton of functionality. This ease of function creates an experience that's calm, minimal, and fun. However, if you've ever visited a cumbersome website with tons of options, flashing banner ads, and movement all over the place, you will most likely want to leave. You'll feel overwhelmed.

The following are a few ways we can incorporate simplicity into our course design:

- Focus on simplicity in visual design. Be sure to use negative space in the layout of your course documents. When creating a slideshow presentation, limit the text per slide and focus on simplifying the language.
- Break text up into bulleted points and lists when addressing multiple ideas.
- Create shorter paragraphs. Students will likely be reading online, where longer paragraphs can be harder to read. By creating shorter paragraphs, students will have an easier time focusing on information. This can also increase accessibility and even work as an accommodation.
- Use visual cues that include consistent icons.
- Make use of short checklists that students can use to stay on track.

When I create slideshows, I use the same consistent visual cues to guide students through the directions. I use groupings on the top left-hand corner. I also have an icon for the activity (a blog post). In the top right-hand corner, I have an icon for the allotted time. All of these visual cues allow students to process the information quickly. In addition, I use a different color for each phase of the lesson, which gives a visual cue that we have transitioned.

INDIVIDUAL

25 MINUTES

BLOG POST

Create your next blog post on your professional educator blog.

Need ideas? Check our collective brainstorming document
on Google Classroom.

For what it's worth, I might be the only professor in our department who sketches out my own icons. If that's not your jam, there are many sites online where you can find simple icons that look professional.

7. SOLICIT FREQUENT FEEDBACK.

There are many ways to solicit student feedback. You might create targeted surveys on a specific area of course design. Other times, you might create a survey about how easy or challenging it was to navigate the course documents. This type of specific feedback can help with course organization, course structure, and course communication. I then modified my systems based on the data trends that I noticed.

As I previously mentioned, you can also solicit feedback by asking students to share their experiences during a student leadership team meeting. You can have students annotate the course documents and insert specific comments and questions to help you clarify expectations. You might pull a small group for a five-minute focus group activity and ask students about a core area of your course design.

CONDUCTING A UX DESIGN AUDIT FOR YOUR COURSE

Throughout this chapter, I have shared specific ideas you can use as you embrace UX design. However, as educators, we are busy. We can't implement every single strategy. Even if we did, we would overwhelm students with too many surveys and interviews. Classrooms are communities and communities are inherently messy and dynamic. However, we can find small ways to embrace UX design so that students have a more seamless learning experience. One way is through a UX design course audit.

The best systems are the ones that feel invisible. You step into it and immediately know where to go and what to do. Don't get me wrong. Confusion can be a great thing in a classroom if it is leading toward deeper learning. But confusion caused by poorly designed courses leads to disengagement and frustration. It cuts learning short and disrupts creative flow.

I am still early on in this journey. However, I am encouraged by the results so far. I've seen huge improvements in my course evaluations in the category of organization. Eventually, I want to get to a place where students aren't even thinking about the course architecture but are so empowered by the learning that they hardly notice that the systems exist. When that happens, I can focus on what truly matters: the critical thinking, the creativity, and the community we are building together.

GREAT DESIGN SHOULD FEEL INVISIBLE

CHAPTER 15

BUILDING A COURSE

In the previous chapter, we explored specific ways to design systems that empower our students. We focused on how you can build structures for clarity and student ownership in hybrid- and distance learning environments. In this chapter, we will focus on how to design a long-term distance learning plan. As educators, we know that we'll need a nimble and iterative approach toward strategic planning.

Our plans will change throughout the year. This is especially true if you are in a remote or hybrid environment due to a pandemic or other unforeseen event. However, the greatest value in planning isn't necessarily in the plans themselves but in the act of planning. Here, you can think strategically, intentionally, and proactively before your course begins so that your approach can be more adaptive as the year progresses.

PHASE 1
CREATE A PERSONAL PLAN

It might seem counterintuitive to focus on a personal plan before designing a plan for your courses. However, the shift toward remote and hybrid learning can be a challenging, disorienting process. Instructors often experience a learning curve in which certain tasks might take longer than in a virtual setting than they would in a face-to-face classroom. For example, you might spend hours creating and editing a video for direct instruction in an online class, while the same process would be a single synchronous lesson in-person. In hybrid courses, it can feel as though you are doing twice the prep work as you plan out activities for students at home and in-person. This added complexity can be mentally exhausting.

Furthermore, teachers and professors often pay an emotional cost as they switch to remote and hybrid learning as well. As the instructor, you might miss out on the big "aha" moments when students finally master a new skill. As a community, we all miss out on the rich, in-the-moment discussions that we have in face-to-face environments. While you can create inside jokes, you miss out on the laughter and the side conversations. You also miss out on those small moments to connect with students in between classes or at the school dances, plays, and sporting events. In addition, teachers in remote-learning environments spend more time answering emails and engaging in administrative tasks.

In many cases, you will be designing new systems and finding new organizational structures. This can feel exhausting. If you think back to your first year of teaching, everything felt new. You often second-guessed your actions, and you constantly focused on finding better approaches to your craft. While this led to significant growth, it's why you also had days when you plowed through a tub of chocolate chip cookie dough ice cream and then fell asleep at six o'clock. Or, maybe that was just me.

As you shift toward remote and hybrid learning, there's a tendency to dream up new ideas and work tirelessly on creating materials for your students. You know what great teaching looks like in person, and you want to make that a reality online as well. You also know that students will be experiencing isolation, and you want to make sure that you connect with them on a relational level. The problem is, if you focus on planning your courses without thinking about your own needs, you can easily spend twelve hours a day doing remote and hybrid teaching and still feel like you're not doing enough.

This is why it helps to start with a personal plan for remote teaching. You have limited time and energy, and you have a life outside of your job. It's not selfish to look out for your social and emotional needs. In fact, it can help prevent burnout and allow you to thrive in your role as a teacher.

The following are certain things you might include in your personal plan:

- **Set realistic expectations for yourself.** Make a list of everything you will do as a teacher and then estimate how long each task takes. Then multiply that times 1.5. We tend to overestimate our ability to accomplish tasks quickly. It's called the planning fallacy. Next, go through the list of expectations and cut out parts that aren't absolutely necessary. You might even pull back on certain things that you know are important but also not feasible given your schedule. For example, you might not be able to do a synchronous video conference with every student each month, but you might be able to meet with each student once per quarter.
- **Create specific boundaries.** When learning can happen anywhere at any time, you can feel the pressure to be available anywhere at any time as well. This why boundaries are critical in remote learning. You might set a specific worktime where you begin and end your day. For example, you might choose to end your day at 5:00 p.m. At that point, you can no longer grade assignments or plan lessons. If possible, you might have a physical workspace and then avoid that space when you have "clocked out" for the day. If that's not possible, you can have a curfew for your computer and choose a specific time when you unplug for the evening. You'll likely need to communicate these expectations to students who might be working late at night or to parents and guardians who send urgent emails. If you are tempted to answer emails after your curfew, you might consider taking your work email off of your phone.
- **Redefine success.** This year will come with significant challenges and epic mistakes. In certain ways, you might feel less effective than in previous years. It can help to redefine success to be about processes rather than results. You might define success as taking creative risks, owning mistakes, and choosing to grow. You might define it as simply being faithful to

your craft, your values, and your identity. This is a shift from viewing as the result of actions to viewing success as the actions themselves. We can't predict how things will turn out. This year will be experimental. However, if we treat failed experiments as learning experiences, we are more likely to stick with it during the challenging moments.

- **Connect with a community.** Find a professional community where you can connect and share ideas. It might be a team of teachers or professors in your department. Or it might be a community where you can connect online and share ideas. Seek out a community that goes beyond venting and into true vulnerability, where each person is sharing their stories, showing empathy, and solving problems together. Earlier, I mentioned the mastermind structure for student feedback. However, you might want to create a teacher mastermind group where you set goals and reflect on progress together.
- **Own your professional learning.** Come up with a plan for finding new ideas and strategies. It might be a short online course or a series of webinars. You might start a curation process of resources. You could do a book study with colleagues. Part of avoiding burnout is finding inspiration and new ideas.

This year will stretch you in new ways. You'll grow in your craft, and you'll learn so many new things. But it's also going to be challenging. By creating a personal plan, you can set necessary parameters that can help you avoid burnout.

SELF-CARE IS STUDENT CARE

YOU CAN'T TEACH
WHEN YOUR BATTERY IS DRAINED

PHASE 2
EXPLORING IDEAS

After creating an initial plan for yourself, it can help to move into a phase where you explore ideas and dream up possibilities and then move into a slower incubation phase where you work and rework ideas. Ideally, this second phase can last for weeks. However, changes can occur quickly, and some educators will need to move quickly through this second phase and schedule time throughout the year to explore ideas.

It helps to start from a place of empathy. Here, you might send out a survey to students and families to get a sense of who they are and what they need. This survey might include questions about technology access, daily schedules, preferences in learning tasks, topics they find interesting, and overall concerns they might have. You could ask students for ideas of activities or projects they might want to pursue. If you have the time and resources, you might conduct interviews with families. If you've developed trust, you can ask students and their parents or guardians to walk you through a day in the life at their home. By starting with empathy, you can search for strategies and materials that are more closely aligned to the needs of your students.

This exploration phase is inherently messy. It's a sandbox space where you can play around with different apps or test out new technology. It's a chance to curate resources you find online. You might create visual curations site or you might organize these resources on a shared document or spreadsheet. This doesn't have to be a solitary endeavor. We tend to think of brainstorming as a small-group activity, but you might brainstorm together with a single partner. In addition, you might connect with educators online to share ideas in a private social media group. As a team or department, you keep a collection of ideas and materials in a shared online folder. After exploring ideas, you can begin to plan out your course. Often, this second phase will morph into the third phase naturally.

PHASE 3
PLANNING YOUR COURSE

There is no set "right method" for planning out a course. Some teachers use whiteboards with diagrams and arrows pointing in every direction. Others cover their wall with sticky notes. Some use arrows and sticky notes, and they begin to look like a character on a crime show trying to explain a bizarre conspiracy theory. However, other teachers and professors simply open up a Word document and type out a linear yearlong plan. Some teachers work collaboratively as a team, while others prefer to plan in solitude.

In general, this third phase starts with a general course outline for the entire semester or year. From there, you develop unit plans that include the learning targets, standards, course materials, activity ideas, assignments, and assessments. Some instructors might even choose to build their course directly into the LMS. Again, this process is deeply personal. Each instructor's approach is different. As you design your yearlong plan, you might also develop a gradual release schedule for student ownership. Here are some key ideas:

- Build ownership into the class norms, rules, and procedures. You might even recruit a student leadership team and invite all students to participate.
- Create opportunities for student feedback in the course design. You might design a student course survey that you send every few weeks. You might also set up a protocol in which students annotate course documents.

- Create a curation of forms, tutorials, and graphic organizers. Visualize how you will teach students to self-select the scaffolds.
- Create student jobs and an application process so students can take active ownership in running the class. You might launch a student technology help team as well.
- Design elements for student ownership in virtual meetings. Find specific ways to make the meetings interactive and hands on, in a way that builds on student agency. It might be a scavenger hunt or a show-and-tell activity. You might have students submit memes or a joke-of-the-day to add some joy and levity to your classroom culture.
- Introduce student choice menus. You might also create a gradual release process where you move through the levels of choice menus with your students.
- Tap into student interests by launching Geek Out Blogs or Genius Hour projects.
- Incorporate student-centered questioning techniques. Do an audit of your lesson plans to see areas where you might encourage students to ask more questions.
- Pilot an inquiry-based mini-project, such as a Wonder Day project, Curiosity Cast, or "What can you do with it?" math problem.
- Engage students in collaborative work. You might take a gradual release approach here with more ownership in things like communication and project management as students spend more time in collaborative groups.
- Launch specific creative projects in which students can own the entire creative process.
- Introduce student-centered assessment practices, including self-assessment and peer assessment.

After thinking through unit plans and the process of ownership, you can begin choosing the platforms and tools. Think through the types of tools students will use for synchronous and asynchronous learning.

A word of caution here: each technology tool or platform has a learning curve for students. Students might spend two or three hours on their first blog post and later knock out a post in twenty minutes. It can also get overwhelming for students and families when there are too many platforms with various logins and passwords. It can help to limit the number of platforms that students will use. This also helps parents and guardians who can feel overwhelmed by the logistical challenges of managing logins and passwords.

In addition, you will also need to make sure that the tools you select comply with district policies and adhere to local and national laws for student privacy and safety. In the United States, teachers might need to doublecheck to see that their tools are COPPA and CIPA compliant. Professors and teachers will need to review whether technology tools comply with FERPA, IDEA, and ADA. In education circles, educators sometimes "ask forgiveness rather than permission." However, with digital policies and laws, the legal system will expect you to comply rather than ask forgiveness. You're better off contacting leadership and clearing your technology tools ahead of time.

In this phase, you might also think through how you will organize your daily classes based on your learning environment. You might be fully online and asynchronous, meaning you have a flexible daily schedule, and you can create optional time slots in which students can meet with you. However, you might have specific, scheduled virtual classes where you will be planning interactive class meetings. You might also be in a hybrid environment, where students meet virtually and online for most days but also meet up in person on certain scheduled days.

Finally, you might develop a community-engagement plan. This plan might include protocols you will use for developing shared norms and procedures as well as specific activities you will use to build community. You can also create a plan for student communication, including how often you will do video updates, emails to the entire class, and individual check-ups. At the K-12 level, you might also set up a plan for communicating with parents and guardians. This might include positive emails home, updates for students missing work, a class newsletter, surveys for direct input, and ways parents or guardians can participate or volunteer virtually.

PHASE 4
BUILDING YOUR COURSE

After planning out your course, you can begin to build the systems. This includes setting up your LMS. Some instructors might build out the entire course on an LMS and schedule all assignments in advance. Others might focus on the first or second unit of the school year. I've found that in hybrid courses, it works best to make each week visible in the LMS on the Friday before the next week. However, for fully online and virtual courses, students respond well to having the entire course available from the start. Ultimately, it's within your discretion.

In this phase, you will also create a course syllabus and develop a course calendar. You might even create your course assignment directions or project instructions. This is also the phase where you narrow down your course materials, such as videos, podcasts, articles, and website links. You might create some of your templates for your weekly emails as a way to streamline communication. Here's where a collaborative team can make a significant difference. As a group, you can divide up tasks so that various team members add resources, design communication templates, and curate tutorials. One member might focus on technology tutorials, another on academic tutorials, and another on language scaffolds.

If you're in a leadership position, please provide educators with the freedom to build out their courses as much as they feel is necessary. Some teachers will spend a few weeks and design a complete course on the LMS. They prefer to film every instructional video and schedule every video conference in advance. These instructors will spend hours in advance engaged in the planning, designing, and revising of course materials. By developing a course in advance, they are better able to engage relationally with students and modify course materials as they go. Other instructors will create a general outline, a syllabus, a course calendar, and an initial first-week unit plan. They prefer to plan as they go based on personal reflection, student assessments, and feedback from student surveys. Both of these approaches work as long as educators are being intentional ahead of time and flexible in the moment.

PHASE 5
REVISING YOUR COURSE

After creating your initial course, you can move into a revision phase. It helps to invite students to provide feedback so you can fine-tune your course materials and modify your systems and structures. The following questions can help guide the process.

- What is your overall perception of this course? How does this compare to your expectations of the course?
- What aspects of this course seem confusing or disorganized?
- What parts of this course work well for you?
- What is missing from this course that you wish were included?
- What parts of this course seem unnecessary?
- What aspects of this course are you most excited about?

You might also invite colleagues to review your course as well. This could include leadership, such as a principal, dean, or director. It might also include coaches or specialists in technology, special education, or language acquisition. At times, you might ask a colleague who has a certain lens to provide a critique. For example, I work with a professor who is an expert in trauma-informed pedagogy, and she has provided helpful feedback on how to improve course consistency and share expectations in a way that is helpful for students who have faced trauma.

You might reach out to certain trusted colleagues and do a course design workshop patterned after the writer's workshop process. Each person opens up their course for fellow teachers to analyze. They then provide constructive feedback, affirmation, and ideas. While this process can sound scary, the mutual feedback keeps it democratic. It's actually led to a deeper trust as a department because we are each sharing from a place of vulnerability.

At times, you might even conduct a larger audit of course design and materials. This audit might be a UX design audit with a focus on student experience. It might be an accessibility audit with a focus on universal design for learning principles. You can reach out to special-education specialists who can help guide you through strategies and policies for increased inclusion. You might also do an equity audit and invite experts in anti-racism and culturally responsive education to identify hidden biases, review cultural representation, critique course systems, and provide suggestions for revisions. These audit processes take time and require a financial commitment. However, they can also work as a form of professional development for educators who are working toward improving their course design.

CONCLUSION

ALWAYS TEACH
IN BETA

"I feel like I'm a new teacher all over again." So many teachers have shared that sentiment in various ways. This shift in teaching approaches can feel bewildering. You're learning so many new skills and discovering new ideas and making entirely new mistakes – which is why you need the New Teacher Card.

When I was a first-year teacher, my team leader Nancy gave me this heaping box of classroom supplies. On the top, she placed a notecard with the words New Teacher Card. On the back of the notecard, she wrote a note explaining that I could play this card when I messed up. "You're new and you make mistakes, but that's okay. Just play the New Teacher Card. Feel free to play this card when you mess up or when you don't know how things work and you need to ask for help. Play this card when you miss a meeting or you don't get every paper graded or you have a day when your lesson fails. This is going to happen often in your first year. But don't beat yourself up. Just play the New Teacher Card and re-member that mistakes are how we learn."

I played that card so many times in my first year. I had cringe-worthy moments when I yelled at a class or shamed a student without realizing it. This New Teacher Card became my go-to every time I felt like an imposter, and I find myself replaying all the mis-takes I've made in thirteen years of teaching. It's the card I play every time I slip into perfectionism.

I've come to believe that this New Teacher Card is something you should never let go of in teaching. Although you grow in knowledge and expertise, you will always remain imperfect.

The New Teacher Card is more than just a forgiveness card. It's a reminder to keep experimenting and trying new strategies and testing out new ideas. The New Teacher Card means you're open to new possibilities. It means you're willing to take creative risks. I've played this card when I first tried out sketch-noting or student blogging. I used it when we painted murals and filmed documentaries. I kept playing it with our Genius Hour projects that started out rocky and ultimately became a student favorite.

The New Teacher Card reminds me that every single lesson is an experiment. It might work. It might fail. But the biggest risk I can take is not taking the risk at all. Think of the New Teacher Card as an invitation to innovation — to rewrite the rules of teaching and to experiment with new ideas and transform your classroom into a bastion of creativity and wonder. Consider it as a chance to move through iterations in small ways and to grow in your craft.

The new teacher card is a reminder that you will make some big mistakes in this shift toward hybrid and remote learning. But for all the failed experiments and moments that don't turn out perfectly, you will have some amazing moments. You'll watch students have deep insights and creative breakthroughs. You'll build an empowered community. Despite the imperfection, amazing things will continue to happen because you are empowering your students regardless of where they are located.

FOOTNOTES

¹ Puentedura, Ruben R. "The SAMR model: Background and exemplars." *Retrieved June 24* (2012): 2013.

² Check out Derek Muller's videos on scientific processes: https://www.youtube.com/user/1veritasium

³ A common example would be Flipgrid

⁴ For a quick primer on Genius Hour, check out AJ Juliani's work: http://ajjuliani.com/genius-hour-blueprint-step-step-guide-running-project-class/

⁵ While there is some debate on who first coined the term "flipped classroom," the concept has been around as early as this:
King, Alison (1993). "From sage on the stage to guide on the side". College Teaching. 41 (1): 30–35. doi:10.1080/87567555.1993.9926781.

⁶ You can find the 20-minute conference / peer feedback system here: http://www.spencerauthor.com/the-20-minute-peer-feedback-system/

⁷ For information on CIPA go to https://www.fcc.gov/consumers/guides/childrens-internet-protection-act

⁸ For information on COPPA go to https://www.ftc.gov/enforcement/rules/rulemaking-regulatory-reform-proceedings/childrens-online-privacy-protection-rule

⁹ Conceptual Metaphor Theory explores the relationships of implied metaphors and the language that we use. You can find more at:
Lakoff, George, and Mark Johnson. "Conceptual metaphor in everyday language." *The journal of Philosophy* 77, no. 8 (1980): 453-486.

¹⁰ I am not an expert on anti-racist education. However, you can find some thoughts and recommended resources on this blog post: http://www.spencerauthor.com/anti-racism-principal/

¹¹ There is a great description of Socratic Seminars in:
Israel, Elfie. "Examining Multiple Perspectives in Literature." In *Inquiry and the Literary Text: Constructing Discussions in the English Classroom.* James Holden and John S. Schmit, eds. Urbana, IL: NCTE, 2002.

¹² It is far more complicated than simply "games are addicting." This article explores the nuances of gaming, participation, and experiences:
Lenhart, Amanda, Joseph Kahne, Ellen Middaugh, Alexandra Rankin Macgill, Chris Evans, and Jessica Vitak. "Teens, Video Games, and Civics: Teens' Gaming Experiences Are Diverse and Include Significant Social Interaction and Civic Engagement." *Pew internet & American life project* (2008).

¹³ Goldstein, Dana, A. Popescu, and N. Hannah-Jones. "As school moves online, many students stay logged out." *New York Times. https://www. nytimes. com/2020/04/06/us/coronavirus-schools-attendance-absent. html* (2020).

¹⁴ Schlechty, P. C. (2002). *Working on the Work: An Action Plan for Teachers, Principals, and Superintendents. The Jossey-Bass Education Series.* Jossey-Bass, 989 Market Street, San Francisco, CA 94103-1741.

¹⁵ Schlechty, Phillip C. *Working on the Work: An Action Plan for Teachers, Principals, and Superintendents. The Jossey-Bass Education Series.* Jossey-Bass, 989 Market Street, San Francisco, CA 94103-1741, 2002.

¹⁶ There's a deeper dive into this topic here:

https://www.pennmedicine.org/news/news-blog/2020/june/coping-with-covid-stress

[17] Pearson, P. D., and G. Gallagher. "The gradual release of responsibility model of instruction." *Contemporary Educational Psychology* 8, no. 3 (1983): 112-123.

[18] See this EdWeek article on the topic: https://blogs.edweek.org/edweek/DigitalEducation/2020/03/school-buses-wifi-hotspots-coronavirus.html

[19] Check out this NPR article on the topic:
https://www.npr.org/2020/03/27/821926032/with-schools-closed-kids-with-disabilities-are-more-vulnerable-than-ever

[20] There is an excellent set of curated resources at bit.ly/ANTIRACISMRESOURCES

[21] There are some definite issues with BYOD and equity:
Fincher, Derrel. "Bring Your Own Device (BYOD) programs in the classroom: teacher use, equity, and learning tools." (2016).

[22] Prensky, Marc. "Digital natives, digital immigrants." *On the horizon* 9, no. 5 (2001).

[23] https://www.ada.gov/cguide.htm

[24] https://sites.ed.gov/idea/

[25] There's an interesting issue of emojis presenting challenges for blind users. Learn more here:
https://www.cbc.ca/radio/spark/381-the-bad-design-behind-hawaii-s-missile-scare-internet-freedom-in-iran-and-more-1.4491385/loudly-crying-face-your-cute-emojis-are-spoiling-social-media-for-blind-users-1.4491393

[26] Grandgeorge, Marine, and Nobuo Masataka. "Atypical color preference in children with autism spectrum disorder." *Frontiers in psychology* 7 (2016): 1976.

[27] There are many different ELL accommodations that can be found in the SIOP® Model:
Vogt, MaryEllen, and Jana Echevarría. *99 ideas and activities for teaching English learners with the SIOP model.* Boston: Pearson Allyn and Bacon, 2008.

[28] Xiong, Jiaqi, Orly Lipsitz, Flora Nasri, Leanna MW Lui, Hartej Gill, Lee Phan, David Chen-Li et al. "Impact of COVID-19 pandemic on mental health in the general population: A systematic review." *Journal of affective disorders* (2020).

[29] Anderson, Terry, and D. Randy Garrison. "Learning in a networked world: New roles and responsibilties." In *Distance Learners in Higher Education: Institutional responses for quality outcomes. Madison, Wi.: Atwood.* 1998.

[30] Gay, Geneva. *Culturally responsive teaching: Theory, research, and practice.* Teachers College Press, 2018.

[31] Page 227 of Gay, Geneva. *Culturally responsive teaching: Theory, research, and practice.* Teachers College Press, 2018.

[32] Dean Shareski's TED Talk can be found here: https://www.youtube.com/watch?v=qd-Nk2sB-vA

[33] This might be Flipgrid, Voxer, or Marco Polo

[34] You can find the templates and examples here: http://www.spencerauthor.com/the-power-of-student-conferencing/

[35] Sariyati, Ice. "The effectiveness of TPR (Total Physical Response) method in English vocabulary mastery of elementary school children." *PAROLE: Journal of Linguistics and Education* 3, no. 1 April (2013): 50-64.

[36] Schwartz, Barry. "The paradox of choice: Why more is less." New York: Ecco, 2004.

[37] Kasey Bell wrote about this here: https://shakeuplearning.com/blog/interactive-learning-menus-choice-boards-using-google-docs/ and Catlin Tucker wrote about it here: https://catlintucker.com/2016/04/design-your-own-digital-choice-board/

[38] While we often think about Google as the origin of 20% Time, it actually existed at 3M decades earlier:

https://www.fastcompany.com/1663137/how-3m-gave-everyone-days-off-and-created-an-innovation-dynamo

[39] Link to Wonder Day at http://www.spencerauthor.com/wonder-week/

[40] This blog post by Kimberly Hellerich includes trauma-sensitive approaches to the start of the school year: https://www.edutopia.org/article/trauma-informed-classroom-strategies

[41] Geek Out Blogs can be found at http://www.spencerauthor.com/geek-out-projects/

[42] E Carpenter, Jeffrey Paul. "Unconference professional development: Edcamp participant perceptions and motivations for attendance." *Professional Development in Education* 42, no. 1 (2016): 78-99.

[43] An education professor had to shut down his entire wiki due to the potential FERPA violations. You can read about it here: https://computinged.wordpress.com/2011/11/15/no-more-swikis-end-of-the-constructionist-web-at-georgia-tech/

[44] An example might be Voxer

[45] This could be something like Flipgrid or Voice Thread

[46] This could include something like Slack

[47] Threaded or unthreaded refers to the type of discussion threads. Here's a primer on the subject:
Kirk, James J., and Robert L. Orr. "A Primer on the Effective Use of Threaded Discussion Forums." (2003).

[48] This might include a tool such as Padlet or Stormboard

[49] There are many different inquiry theorists, though some people view it as a pedagogical structure rather than a learning theory.

[50] Banchi, Heather, and Randy Bell. "The many levels of inquiry." *Science and children* 46, no. 2 (2008): 26.

[51] Dan Meyer has done a great TED Talk on this topic of doing a "math makeover" https://www.ted.com/talks/dan_meyer_math_class_needs_a_makeover?language=en

[52] 'Mythbusters'. 2007. TV programme. Discovery channel.

[53] There are actually multiple science fairs, including https://www.societyforscience.org/isef/ and https://www.competitionsciences.org/competitions/google-science-fair/

[54] National History Day can be found at https://www.nhd.org/

[55] A great tool is Audacity

[56] Rowling, J. K. *Harry Potter and the Sorcerer's Stone*. New York: Arthur A. Levine Books, 1998.

[57] Collins, Suzanne. 2008. *The Hunger Games*. New York, New York: Scholastic Press.

[58] This American Life can be found at https://www.thisamericanlife.org/ and RadioLab can be found at https://www.wnycstudios.org/podcasts/radiolab

[59] Harford, T. (2017). *Fifty things that made the modern economy*. Hachette UK.

[60] They can do this on PowerPoint, Keynote, or Google Slides.

[61] Banchi, Heather, and Randy Bell. "The many levels of inquiry." *Science and children* 46, no. 2 (2008): 26.

[62] Meyer, Daniel Z., Joy Kubarek-Sandor, James Kedvesh, Cheryl Heitzman, Yaozhen Pan, and Sima Faik. "Eight ways to do inquiry." *The Science Teacher* 79, no. 6 (2012): 40.

[63] Pedaste, Margus, Mario Mäeots, Leo A. Siiman, Ton De Jong, Siswa AN Van Riesen, Ellen T. Kamp, Constantinos C. Manoli, Zacharias C. Zacharia, and Eleftheria Tsourlidaki. "Phases of inquiry-based learning: Definitions and the inquiry cycle." *Educational research review* 14 (2015): 47-61.

[64] Jonassen, David H., Joost Lowyck, and Thomas M. Duffy, eds. *Designing environments for constructive learning*. Springer-Verlag, 1993.

65 Jacoby, Barbara. *Service-learning essentials: Questions, answers, and lessons learned.* John Wiley & Sons, 2014.

66 Ravitz, Jason. "Beyond changing culture in small high schools: Reform models and changing instruction with project-based learning." *Peabody Journal of Education* 85, no. 3 (2010): 290-312.

67 Mergendoller, John R., Thom Markham, Jason Ravitz, and John Larmer. "Pervasive Management of Project Based Learning: Teachers as Guides and Facilitators." (2006).

68 Pellegrino, James W., and Margaret L. Hilton. "Committee on defining deeper learning and 21st century skills." *Center for Education* (2012).

69 Bell, Stephanie. "Project-based learning for the 21st century: Skills for the future." *The clearing house* 83, no. 2 (2010): 39-43.

70 Grant, Michael M. "Getting a grip on project-based learning: Theory, cases and recommendations." *Meridian: A middle school computer technologies journal* 5, no. 1 (2002): 83. Larmer, John, John R. Mergendoller, and Suzie Boss. "Gold standard PBL: Essential project design elements." *Buck Institute for Education* (2015): 1-4.

71 Mergendoller, J. R., Markham, T., Ravitz, J., & Larmer, J. (2006). Pervasive Management of Project Based Learning: Teachers as Guides and Facilitators.

72 Larmer, John, and John R. Mergendoller. "Seven essentials for project-based learning." *Educational leadership* 68, no. 1 (2010): 34-37.

73 Divergent thinking was a term coined by JP Guilford: Guilford, J.P. (1988). Some changes in the structure of intellect model. *Educational and Psychological Measurement, 48,* 1-4.

74 *The Definitive Guide to Project Management.* Nokes, Sebastian. 2nd Ed.n. London (Financial Times / Prentice Hall): 2007. ISBN 978-0-273-71097-4

75 The metacognition cycle can be found in: Ambrose, S. A., Bridges, M. W., DiPietro, M., Lovett, M. C., & Norman, M. K. (2010). *How learning works: Seven research-based principles for smart teaching.* John Wiley & Sons.

76 Pardo, Catherine Vanessa, and Cecilia Cisterna. "Cell Phone Screen Recording App: an Effective Tool to Enhance English Language Fluency." *Colombian Applied Linguistics Journal* 21, no. 2 (2019).

77 This phenomenon is explored in: Buckingham, M., & Goodall, A. (2019). The feedback fallacy. *Harvard Business Review, 97*(2), 92-101.

And in their book: Buckingham, M., & Goodall, A. (2019). *Nine lies about work: A freethinking leader's guide to the real world.* Harvard Business Press.

78 See-think-wonder originated as a thinking strategy from Project Zero: https://pz.harvard.edu/resources/see-think-wonder. You can also find it in: Ritchhart, R., Church, M., & Morrison, K. (2011). *Making thinking visible: How to promote engagement, understanding, and independence for all learners.* John Wiley & Sons.

79 Feedback carousel was originated by Kagan Learning: Kagan, S., & Kagan, M. (2009). *Kagan Cooperative Learning.* San Clemente: Kagan Publishing.

80 A great primer on UX Design is: Schmidt, Aaron, and Amanda Etches. *Useful, usable, desirable.* 2014.

81 The idea of UX Design is not the same as LX Design. However, LX Design takes many ideas from UX Design: Kalyuga, Slava, Paul Chandler, and John Sweller. "Incorporating learner experience into the design of multimedia instruction." *Journal of educational psychology* 92, no. 1 (2000): 126.

DR. JOHN SPENCER

Dr. John Spencer is a former middle school teacher and current college professor on a on a quest to see teachers unleash the creative potential in all of their students. He regularly explores research, interviews educators, deconstructs systems, and studies real-world examples of student empowerment in action. He shares these insights in books, blog posts, journal articles, free resources, animated videos, and podcasts.

In Spencer's second year of teaching, he launched a student-centered documentary project. He spent the next decade on a journey to empower his students to become creative thinkers and problem-solvers. This meant mural projects, service-learning projects, designing STEM camps, and creating coding projects.

He is the co-author of the bestselling books *Launch* and *Empower*. In 2013, he spoke at the White House, sharing a vision for how to empower students to be future-ready through creativity and design thinking. Spencer has led workshops and delivered keynotes around the world with a focus on student creativity and self-direction. He frequently works with schools, districts, and organizations on how to design student-centered learning in blended, hybrid, and remote learning environments.

Email: john@spencerauthor.com
Website: spencerauthor.com
Twitter: @spencerideas
YouTube: spencervideos.com
Instagram: @spencereducation

BRING JOHN SPENCER TO YOUR SCHOOL OR EVENT

Dr. Spencer offers a creative, thought-provoking, and humorous style through his keynotes, full-day workshops and online professional development. He offers the unique perspective of being a published author, the co-founder of a successful startup, an award-winning classroom teacher, and a college professor. He uses this blend of classroom experience, industry experience, and research experience to craft innovative, holistic, and practical learning experiences in a style that is approachable and relevant.

Check it out at: http://www.spencerauthor.com/speaking-and-consulting/

DISTANCE LEARNING WORKSHOPS

As a technology coach and STEM teacher, Spencer helped lead his district in blended and virtual options. As a university professor, he has worked as a Digital Fluency Initiative mentor, provided professional development on course design, and helped professors transform their face-to-face courses into distance learning courses. Spencer's style is hands-on, engaging, practical, and fun; infusing each learning experience with storytelling, humor, and movement. While he tailors the learning to the needs of your staff, here is a sampling of the workshops he leads.

Better by Design: How to Empower Students in Virtual and Distance Learning Environments

We didn't ask for this. We didn't anticipate this. But now many of us are teaching online and virtually. In this workshop, we explore how to boost engagement, improve collaboration, and increase student ownership in distance learning environments. We explore, step-by-step, how to improve virtual class meetings, how to use choice menus strategically, and how to get students engaged in creative projects at home. By the end, you'll have tools, strategies, and a clear plan for the future.

Boosting Student Engagement Online

In this workshop, we cover seven specific strategies you can use to boost student engagement when doing virtual sessions. We dive into how to create meaningful small group interaction and how to incorporate movement and creativity into these sessions. We also explore how to design meaningful online instruction that takes students away from their screens.

Creative Collaboration from a Distance

Distance learning does not mean you have to abandon collaborative grouping. In this session, we explore how to build accountability and interdependency into student collaboration. We cover specific tools you can use for shared creative work and for both synchronous and asynchronous communication.

Taking Distance Learning to the Next Level

In this workshop, we focus on how to take our distance learning to the next level with UX Design. We explore what it means to do in-depth choice menus, project-based learning units, and interdependent collaborative work. This is ideal for schools that have already been experimenting with virtual and distance learning platforms and want to take the learning to another level.

Getting Started with Hybrid Learning

This workshop walks participants step-by-step through the five different hybrid teaching models. Each participant develops a specific hybrid plan along with a sample lesson and a classroom management plan.

Self-Paced Course: Empowering Students in Distance Learning

What does it mean to empower our students in distance learning environments? How do we help them become self-directed when they are away from their classroom? We tackle these hard questions as we focus on what it means to have students self-select scaffolds, use choice menus, engage in creative projects and self-assess. Each day, you will watch a practical video with specific strategies and then create something meaningful that you will actually use in your distance learning classroom.

Made in the USA
Monee, IL
16 October 2020